Dr. Faustus

THE NEW MERMAIDS

General editor: Brian Gibbons
Professor of English Literature, University of Münster

THE NEW MERMAIDS

Dr Faustus

CHRISTOPHER MARLOWE

Edited by
ROMA GILL, OBE

Second edition
based on the A text

LONDON / A & C BLACK

NEW YORK / W W NORTON

Second edition 1989
Reprinted in 1990, 1991, 1993,
1994, 1995
by A & C Black (Publishers) Limited
35 Bedford Row, London WC1R 4JH
ISBN 0-7136-3231-3

First edition in this form 1968
by Ernest Benn Limited

Published in the United States of America by
W. W. Norton and Company, Inc.
500 Fifth Avenue, New York, N.Y. 10110
ISBN 0-393-90059-2 (USA)

Printed in Great Britain by
Whitstable Litho Printers Ltd.,
Whitstable, Kent

CONTENTS

IN MEMORY
OF
MY MOTHER

PREFACE

NOWADAYS IT IS generally recognised that plays, more than any other literary artefacts, are 'unstable' — that is to say, their texts are subject to constant revision and re-revision throughout their theatrical lives. Changes in personnel and politics have their effects on acting companies and, inevitably, on the plays that these produce. Alterations are made to texts, with or without — and sometimes in spite of — the dramatist's consent or even knowledge. The resignation of Edward Alleyn in 1602, and the censorious Act of Abuses in 1606, had remarkable consequences for *Dr Faustus*. There now exist *two* plays of this title! The later play, that represented by the B text of 1616, is not without interest and merit; but it must be recognised that the A text (1604), being less dilute, contains proportionately more of the work of Christopher Marlowe.

In 1964, when I started my work on *Dr Faustus*, it was still thought that the A text was merely an inferior version of the play more accurately presented in the B text. Consequently, the first New Mermaid edition (published in 1965) was based on B. This new edition is very different from its predecessor, but it offers, I believe, something more like the play that Marlowe wrote. The seventeenth-century additions, which were allowed to obscure the dramatist's design, have been removed to the Appendix. The resulting text is shorter and more dramatic; it is 'Elizabethan' rather than 'Jacobean'; and its meaning, although no simpler, is quite uncompromising. It is also a better play.   *October 1994*

ABBREVIATIONS

I HAVE FOLLOWED the usual practice in referring to the seventeenth-century editions of *Dr Faustus*: 'A' indicates substantial agreement between all the A Texts, which are referred to separately on occasion as A1 (1604), A2 (1609), and A3 (1611); the B texts (1616, 1619, 1620, 1624, 1628, and 1631) are similarly distinguished. Modern editions are referred to as follows:

Boas	*The Tragical History of Doctor Faustus*, edited by F. S. Boas (1932)
Bullen	*The Works of Christopher Marlowe*, edited by A. H. Bullen (1885)
Dyce	*The Complete Works of Christopher Marlowe*, edited by A. Dyce (1850)
Greg	*Marlowe's Dr Faustus' 1604–1616: Parallel Texts*, edited by W. W. Greg (1950)
Jump	*Dr Faustus*, edited by John D. Jump (1962)

Other works frequently referred to are:

EFB	*The English Faust Book*, the name given to Marlowe's source [*The Historie of the damnable life, and deserved death of Doctor Iohn Faustus*, translated by P. F. (1592)]
Kocher	P. H. Kocher, *Christopher Marlowe* (Chapel Hill, 1946)

Names of periodicals are abbreviated:

E.L.H.	*English Literary History*
E.S.	*English Studies*
E & S	*Essays and Studies*
M.L.N.	*Modern Language Notes*
M.L.Q.	*Modern Language Quarterly*
M.L.R.	*Modern Language Review*
N & Q	*Notes and Queries*
P.Q.	*Philological Quarterly*
R.E.S.	*Review of English Studies*
T.L.S.	*Times Literary Supplement*

Quotations from other plays by Marlowe are taken from *The Plays of Christopher Marlowe*, edited by Roma Gill (1971); those from Shakespeare's plays are from the Riverside edition.

INTRODUCTION

THE AUTHOR

AT THE AGE OF twenty-nine Marlowe was murdered. His death was welcomed by Her Majesty's Privy Council, which later pardoned the murderer, and by certain popular moralists who hailed it as 'a manifest sign of God's judgement'[1] on a life of impiety and debauchery.

Marlowe was born into a turbulent Canterbury family. His father was a shoemaker of modest means and excessive pugnacity, while two of his sisters, Dorothy and Ann, were notorious in the town – the former for various trade and matrimonial intrigues, the latter a noted 'scold, common swearer and blasphemer of the name of God'.[2] Marlowe escaped from the family environment with the aid of those charitable Elizabethans who had endowed scholarships for the encouragement of learning in poor boys. The first scholarship, of £4 a year, took him to the King's School, Canterbury, from where he proceeded to Cambridge as a Matthew Parker scholar at Corpus Christi College. The Parker scholarship was awarded for three years in the first instance, and might be extended for a further three on evidence that the holder intended to take Holy Orders. Marlowe held his for the full six years. The College's Buttery Book shows him as an undergraduate whose expenditure easily exceeded his income but who from time to time spent nothing at all. There were, evidently, frequent and prolonged absences from Cambridge, and these gave the University cause to question his activities and to threaten, in 1587, to withold his final degree. But Marlowe had strings to pull. A letter from the Privy Council, with the overruling authority of, among others, Archbishop Whitgift, Sir Christopher Hatton, and Lord Burghley, explained in veiled hints the reason for these absences: Marlowe 'had done Her Majestie good service, and deserved to be rewarded for his faithfull dealinge'.[3] He probably went abroad – perhaps to visit the English Catholics at Rheims. Amidst much speculation one

---

[1] Thomas Beard, *Theatre of God's Judgements* (1597), ch. xxv
[2] See William Urry, 'Marlowe and Canterbury', *T.L.S.* (13 February 1964)
[3] Privy Council Register, xxix° Junij 1587; for a full documentation of Marlowe's life and death see J. Leslie Hotson, *The Death of Christopher Marlowe* (1925) and John Bakeless, *The Tragicall History of Christopher Marlowe* (Harvard, 1945)

thing is clear: this 'good service' was not of the kind that is officially recorded and recognised.

A secret agent with an M.A. degree, Marlowe left Cambridge for London. There he consorted with playwrights, at one time sharing a room with Thomas Kyd, author of *The Spanish Tragedy*; quite possibly he associated also with the group of young intellectuals led by Sir Walter Raleigh. Although the facts of his life are largely unknown, its tenor is certain. Arrested once on a charge of homicide, bound over at another time to keep the peace, Marlowe emerges from contemporary legal documents as a rash and fearless quarreller. Mario Praz calls him a *libertin*, using the word to mean both 'free-thinker' and, with its accumulated secondary meaning, 'man of loose morals'.[1] For the free-thinking there is ample evidence of surprising consistency. Richard Baines libelled Marlowe only a few days after the murder. The now famous libel[2] accuses the dramatist of blaspheming the Bible and mocking the state, reporting him as having said:

> ... That the first beginning of Religion was only to keep men in awe ...
> ... That Christ was a bastard and his mother dishonest ...
> ... that all the new testament is filthily written ...

and

> ... that he had as good Right to Coine as the Queen of England.

This last accusation is now supported by a recently-discovered letter from the governor of Flushing, which was sent to Lord Burghley in January 1602. It speaks of the involvement of Marlowe with Baines (who was a petty informer) and a goldsmith, and of an arrest at Flushing when Marlowe and the goldsmith were accused of 'coining'. But the governor, Robert Sidney, clearly has no faith in this charge:

> ... a dutch shilling was uttred, and els not any peece ... the metal is plain peuter and with half an ey to be discovered.[3]

Sir Robert cannot explain the presence of Marlowe in the Netherlands, or his relationship with Baines; but one obvious deduction is that Marlowe's shadowy connection with Her Majesty's secret service did not come to an end when he left Cambridge.

---

[1] 'Christopher Marlowe', *E.S.*, XIII (1931)
[2] MS Harley 6648, ff. 185–6
[3] See R. B. Wernham, 'Christopher Marlowe at Flushing in 1592', *E.H.R.*, XCI (April, 1976), pp. 344–5

Baines continued his libel with the information that whatever the company he came into, Marlowe persuaded its members to atheism,

> willing them not to be afeared of bugbears and hobgoblins, and utterly scorning both god and his ministers.

Marlowe sounds alternately like a perky undergraduate and like a man of plain common sense. But this is a twentieth-century view. To the Elizabethans, fearing for the sanctity of their church and the security of their state, these were 'monstruous opinions', menacing heresies. A warrant was issued for Marlowe's arrest, on evidence supplied perhaps by his former friend Kyd. Kyd himself had been arrested, accused of inciting mob violence and race riots against the Flemish protestants who were then settling in England. Under torture he broke down, and in two letters to Sir John Puckering, the Lord Keeper, he charged Marlowe with heresy and blasphemy.

Before the warrant could be executed Marlowe was killed. The inquest report tells of a squalid encounter in a Deptford tavern on 30 May 1593. Marlowe spent the day there with three 'gentlemen', talking and walking in the garden. But in the evening a quarrel was struck up over who should pay the bill, '*le recknynge*', and in the scuffle that followed Marlowe drew his dagger and wounded one of his companions. The man, Ingram Frizar, snatched the weapon and

> in defence of his life, with the dagger aforesaid of the value of 12d. gave the said Christopher then & there a mortal wound over his right eye of the depth of two inches & of the width of one inch; of which mortal wound the aforesaid Christopher Morley then & there instantly died.[1]

The coroner's account puts a good face on the matter. Yet Ingram Frizar and one, if not both, of his accomplices had connections in some uncertain way with the secret service. Their past histories, and the speed with which, one month later, Frizar was granted a free pardon for the murder, suggest that the 'recknynge' settled in the Deptford tavern was an old score, and probably connected with Marlowe's secret service career.

Marlowe's contemporaries accepted the story of the brawl, but only one seems to have known its ostensible cause. Shakespeare's reference to Marlowe's death serves as an epitaph of his life, the brief life of his most brilliant colleague whose achievement, in five years, is second only to Shakespeare's own:

> A great reckoning in a little room
> *As You Like It*, III, iii, 11

---

[1] Chancery Miscellanea, Bundle 64, File 8, No. 2416 (translated from the Latin)

THE PLAY

Date and Text

Marlowe's reputation rests on four great plays: *Tamburlaine* (in two parts), 1587–8; *The Jew of Malta*, 1590; *Edward II*, 1592; and *Dr Faustus*. At Cambridge Marlowe wrote translations of the Latin poets Lucan and Ovid, and also (perhaps) the early play *Dido Queen of Carthage* – which is a dramatic rendering (and translation) of Book VI of Virgil's *Aeneid*. Another play, *The Massacre at Paris*, was written at about the same time as *The Jew of Malta*: on a political and topical theme, it was popular in the theatre, but the mangled text in which it survives makes critical discussion almost impossible. A different work was *Hero and Leander*, an epic poem of great delight which seems to have been written late in Marlowe's short literary career and which is full of promise for a great future.

The proud-paced verse of *Tamburlaine* stormed the English stage. For his first public theme Marlowe took the story of a peasant warrior whose aspiring mind impelled him to conquest. Over a map of the world, drawn with detailed accuracy from Ortelius' *Theatrum Orbis Terrarum*, Marlowe played 'a great game of chess with kings and conquerors for pieces'.[1] Barabas, protagonist of *The Jew of Malta*, is the reverse of Tamburlaine; schemes of grandeur delight him less than grotesquely comic revenge plots to poison a whole convent of nuns. Far from striding across the known world in the majesty of power, he huddles in his counting-house, accumulating from all quarters of the globe 'Infinite riches in a little room'. King Edward lacks even this ambition, longing only for the 'nook or corner' which all England cannot afford where he may indulge his love for Gaveston. 'Marlowe's mighty line' (the description is Ben Jonson's[2]) is restrained in *Edward II*, but what seems like a loss in energy is compensated by a gain in human feeling.

None of Marlowe's plays can be dated with precision – and *Dr Faustus* is no exception. It had not been performed before the dramatist died in 1593; and although the Admiral's Men staged the other plays in the months immediately following the assassination (perhaps hoping to benefit from the publicity), *Dr Faustus* does not enter the repertoire until 30 September 1594, when the impresario Philip Henslowe recorded in his Diary[3] the fact that he had

Rd at docter ffostose ....iij^{li} xij^s.

(p. 24)

---

[1] Ethel Seaton, 'Marlowe's Map', *E & S*, X (1924), p. 35
[2] line 30 of his memorial verses to Shakespeare, published in the First Folio
[3] *Henslowe's Diary*, ed. R. A. Foakes and R. T. Rickert (1961)

The sum was large – greater than that taken at any other performance the same year; and further entries in the *Diary* testify to the play's continued popularity.

Dr Faustus remained unpublished until the seventeenth century – it was in the actors' own interests not to release the manuscript of their play to a publisher. On 7 January 1601 it was entered in the Stationers' Register:

> Tho. Busshell Entred for his copye under the handes. of Mr Docter Barlowe, and the Warden. A booke called the plaie of Doctor Faustus.

This, I suspect, was merely a 'blocking entry', giving notice of the printer's intention and not resulting immediately in an edition of the play. The first known edition is that of 1604, which was reprinted in 1609 and again in 1611; this is known as the A Text, to distinguish it from the very different B Text, an edition published in 1616 and reprinted several times thereafter. The titlepage of B2 (1619) advertises that the play is 'With new Additions' – a piece of information that ought to have been given three years earlier.

Marlowe's play was altered in 1602: Henslowe's *Diary* records the financial details:

> Lent unto the companye the 22 of november 1602
> to paye unto w^m Bvrde & Samwell Rowle   iiij^{li}
> for ther adicyones in docter fostes the some of
>
> (p. 206)

Such costly 'adicyones' must have been extensive. Perhaps Henslowe felt that *Dr Faustus*, although still a popular play, was somewhat old-fashioned in style, unsuited to modern – i.e. Jacobean – tastes. Furthermore, Henslowe's son-in-law and theatrical partner, the actor Edward Alleyn, was planning to leave the company. He had acted major roles such as Tamburlaine, Barabas, and Faustus; and he would not be easy to replace. A re-writing of the play would modernize it, and also add new interest to compensate for the loss of the leading performer. This is mere speculation, of course – an attempt to explain the problem created by the two texts of *Dr Faustus*.

The A Text, published in 1604
The B Text, published in 1616

B is not only longer and more diffuse than A; the play has also been subjected to severe censorship to satisfy a strict statute, the Act of Abuses, which became law in 1606:

An Acte to restraine Abuses of Players

... That if at any tyme or tymes ... any person or persons doe or shall in any Stage play ... jestingly or prophanely speake or use the holy Name of

God or of Christ Jesus, or of the Holy Ghoste or of the Trinitie, which are not to be spoken but with feare and reverence, shall forfeite for everie such Offence by hym or them committed Tenne Pounde.

The final soliloquy has lost much of its power in the B Text, where a worried Faustus has no vision of Christ's blood streaming in the firmament, and thinks to 'leap up to heaven', rather than (like the A Faustus) 'to my God'.

Until the middle of the twentieth century it was usual to accept the A Text as being closer to Marlowe's original intention because closer in time to his writing. But the efforts of certain scholars – notably Boas, Kirschbaum, and Greg – succeeded in discrediting A as a 'Bad Quarto' (probably a reporter's account of a shortened version of the play) and promoting the B Text as a 'Good Quarto' (based, according to Greg, on Marlowe's 'foul papers'). Greg's argument was ingenious and influential – but unnecessary: there is very little wrong with the A Text, whereas B seems to be based on a copy of A3 augmented by a theatrical manuscript which has been 'edited' by a book-keeper, censored in accordance with the Act of Abuses, and altered by the two dramatists referred to in Henslowe's *Diary*.

The present edition, then, takes A as its copy-text; readings from B are accepted when all of the surviving impressions of A (1604, 1609, and 1611) are manifestly deficient or erroneous.

But what kind of MS was printer's copy for the A Text? Sixteen months elapsed between the dramatist's death and the appearance of his play on the stage – and I suggest that so much time was needed to find some way of completing Marlowe's unfinished work. Some of *Dr Faustus* – the beginning and the end – is in Marlowe's finest style. The mighty line echoes through the first and last soliloquies; it is heard again in the Scholars' praise of Helen and Faustus' own apostrophe to the vision. But the comedy does not seem to be that of the author of *The Jew of Malta* and *The Massacre at Paris*, whose humour is cool, witty, and even cruel. The Prologue to Part 1 of *Tamburlaine* was scornful of contemporary theatrical practice and the crude 'conceits that clownage keeps in pay' – but such 'conceits', the stock-in-trade of Elizabethan clowns, occupy the central scenes of *Dr Faustus* and bridge the twenty-four year gap between the signing of the infernal contract and its expiry date.

Perhaps Marlowe was not interested in the central part of the narrative which was the source for his play; certainly the episodes become repetitive and tedious as the *Faustbook* degenerates into a collection of jests interspersed with moralizing tracts. The comic scenes in the play, however, are not all of a piece. Scenes 2 and 4 appear to be the work of some university wit – perhaps Thomas Nashe – who develops the featureless choric presenter of the

Prologue into the character of Wagner. Wagner is allowed almost a solo performance before the bewildered Scholars, but when he attempts to imitate Faustus and enrol the Clown in his service, it is the Clown who takes possession of the scene, demonstrating different comedy routines which were stock dramatic numbers – the conceits of clownage. The actor who played the Clown in *Dr Faustus* must also have had the role of the clown, known as Adam, in *A Looking Glass for London*, written by Lodge and Greene, and entered in the Stationers' Register in March 1594: he freely transposed lines between this play and *Dr Faustus*. In *A Looking Glass* the Clown, threatened by the devil, attacks with his 'cudgell' until the devil pleads for mercy, when Adam boasts

> Then I may count my selfe I thinke a tall man, that am able to kill a diuell. Now who dare deale with me in the parish, or what wench in *Ninivie* will not loue me, when they say, there goes he that beate the diuell.
>
> G3ᵛ

The lines are introduced into *Dr Faustus* (Scene 4) when Wagner invokes the devils to threaten his reluctant servant, but now the Clown only entertains the possibility of beating the devil: since the lines do not arise directly out of the dramatic situation, it is certain that Marlowe's play must be the borrower.

The *Looking Glass* lines were not the Clown's only contribution. It is very tempting to identify this character with the comic actor, John Adams, who played with Sussex's Men in 1576, and with The Queen's Men in 1583 and 1588.[1] His reputation was good enough to link him with Richard Tarlton in the memory of the Stage-keeper in Jonson's *Bartholmew Fair* when he remembers how

> Adams, the rogue, ha' leaped and capered upon him [Tarlton], and ha' dealt his vermin about as though they had cost him nothing.
>
> (Induction, ll.38–40)

Adams must have been the sort of clown who relied upon a single gimmick – having 'one sute of jeasts, as a man is known by one sute of Apparell' (Q1 *Hamlet*, III,ii). Adams' 'sute of jeasts' – the stage business with fleas – served unusually well for *Dr Faustus*, where the Clown's familiar vermin ('as bold with my flesh as if they had paid for my meat and drink') – enact the diabolic threat to Faustus: 'If thou repent, devils will tear thee in pieces'.

[1] Cf. E. K. Chambers, *Elizabethan Stage* (1923), ii, 296

The Source

THE

HISTORIE

of the damnable
life, and deserved death of
Doctor John Faustus,
Newly imprinted, and in conveni-
ent places imperfect matter amended:
according to the true Copie printed
at Franckfort, *and translated into
English by* P. F. *Gent.*[1]

Stories of witchcraft and enchantment, wandering loose in men's minds, attached themselves in the early sixteenth century to a real-life Georg or Johannes Faustus, scholar and reputed magician of no fixed abode. After this man's death – which gave rise to the most fantastic story of all – his fabled doings were assembled in a 'biography' published in Frankfurt in 1587. The book caught the eye of an Englishman and, translated, was an immediate success. Nothing, not even the name, is known of the translator, P. F. *Gent.* Whoever he was, P. F. shared the German author's staunchly protestant outlook. At some time, however, he must have toured Italy, and because of his efforts to turn the pious jestbook into a Blue Guide we can be certain that Marlowe used the English translation and not the German original. The German, for instance, makes only passing reference to Venice, whereas P. F. remarks the Piazza San Marco and 'the sumptuous Church standing therein called Saint *Markes*'. Marlowe even adds a further detail, although this must be supplied only from his own imagination:

> In midst of which a sumptuous temple stands,
> That threats the stars with her aspiring top.

More intelligent than either of his predecessors, Marlowe had more respect for his hero. No longer the conjuror and calendar-maker of the source, this Faustus is a scholar of distinction. Marlowe's own learning went to the creation of his protagonist, and the verse of the play is heavily encrusted with references to texts that the Cambridge undergraduate must have studied.

Marlowe's source is the subject of a sensitively imaginative study by William Empson, *Faust and the Censor* (1987).

[1] British Museum, C.27.b.43

The Tragedy

The Tragical History
of
the life and death
of
DR FAUSTUS

Boundless in its aspirations, unceasing in its compulsions, the Renaissance mind is the theme of all Marlowe's plays:

> Our souls, whose faculties can comprehend
> The wondrous architecture of the world,
> And measure every wand'ring planet's course,
> Still climbing after knowledge infinite,
> And always moving as the restless spheres,
> Wills us to wear ourselves and never rest...
> *1 Tamburlaine*, II, vii, 21–6

Dr Faustus, the first figure on the English stage who deserves to be called a character, is the epitome of Renaissance aspiration. He has all the divine discontent, the unwearied and unsatisfied striving after knowledge that marked the age in which Marlowe wrote. An age of exploration, its adventurers were not only the merchants and seamen who sailed round the world, but also the scientists, astronomers who surveyed the heavens with their 'optic glass', and those scholars who travelled in the realms of gold to bring back tales of a mighty race of gods and heroes in ancient Greece and Rome. The first soliloquy is 'no mere reckoning of accounts but an inventory of the Renaissance mind'.[1] Faustus is one of the new men. For him, as for Marlowe, lowly birth was no bar to a university education; and as he sits alone in his study reading from the Latin textbooks, he is linked in a common language with scholars from Oxford, Cambridge, and all over the civilized world. Rhetoric, jurisprudence, and medicine have trained a mind apt for questioning, eager for learning, and reluctant to take on trust even the most elementary facts, let alone those hypotheses incapable of empirical proof. The Faustus who refuses to accept from Mephastophilis the evidence for hell's existence is true to himself. His pitiful shortsightedness is all too evident, but there is also a determination to believe only what he himself can prove. This has made him the distinguished scholar he is, the man whose triumphant cry '*sic probo*' has echoed his fame through the German universities. Men of Faustus' calibre were not unknown to Marlowe's age. They were valuable, and they were dangerous. Representative were Sir Walter

[1] Harry Levin, *Christopher Marlowe: the Overreacher* (1954, 2nd ed. 1965), p. 134

Raleigh and his friends, meeting together to discuss philosophy, to debate religion, and to gaze at the stars through Thomas Heriot's new telescope. They attracted much unwanted attention, with accusations of witchcraft and devil-worship. James VI, piously warning his Scottish subjects against the deceits of the devil, observed that those attracted to black magic were, more often than not, men

> having attained to a great perfection in learning, & yet remaining overbare (alas) of the spirit of regeneration and frutes thereof: finding all naturall things common, aswell to the stupid pedants as unto them, they assaie to vendicate unto them a greater name, by not onlie knowing the course of things heavenlie, but likewise to clim to the knowledge of things to come thereby.
>
> *Daemonologie* (Edinburgh, 1597), p. 10

The more man discovered about the universe and his place in it, the more imperative it became for Authority to stress the dangers inherent in the pursuit of knowledge. The wrath of the Almighty and the threat of eternal damnation were powerful deterrents.

The soliloquy with which the play opens should not be read as the random notions of a single idle moment; rather, it is the utterance of thoughts that have been formulating for years in Faustus' mind. He stands at the frontiers of knowledge. The whole of Renaissance learning is within his grasp, but on closer scrutiny of the parts the whole crumbles away and he is left with nothing but a handful of dust. Nothing in the great university curriculum can overcome the melancholy fact – 'Yet art thou still but Faustus, and a man' (Scene 1, line 23). Faustus shares with Hamlet, equally a product of Wittenberg scepticism, this perception of man's paradoxical nature:

> What a piece of work is a man! how noble in reason! how infinite in faculties! ... the beauty of the world, the paragon of animals! And yet, to me, what is this quintessence of dust?
>
> *Hamlet*, II, ii, 293–7

It is this that gives rise to the irony that is the characteristic mode of the play: Faustus begins by longing to be more than human; he ends by imploring metamorphosis into the sub-human. Incidental ironies have a sharp impact within this structure – as when Faustus seals his deed of blood with the last words of Christ on the cross: '*Consummatum est*' (Scene 5, line 74). The impassioned appeal

> Ah Christ my Saviour, seek to save
> Distressed Faustus' soul
>
> Scene 5, lines 257–8

is answered by the emergence of the infernal trinity looking, as J. B. Steane comments, like 'the party bosses in a totalitarian state before

one guilty of thought-crime'.[1] Certain words, frequently reiterated,
carry an ambivalence that points to this initial paradox. Both
cunning and *conceit* were at a semantic crossroads when Marlowe
wrote. The translator of the Psalms could write, for the Authorized
Version, 'If I forget thee, O Jerusalem, let my right hand forget her
cunning' (Ps. 137) at much the same time as Bacon gave the
definition 'We take cunning for a sinister and crooked wisdom'.[2]
Marlowe plays delicately with both meanings, often balancing the
older usage against the newer:

> Till, swollen with cunning, of a self conceit.
>
> Prologue, line 20

Neither *cunning* nor *conceit*, however, has the force Marlowe can
give to the simple word *man*. Faustus envisages a world of power
and delight which 'Stretcheth as far as doth the mind of man'
(Scene 1, line 61). Human potential is set against human limitation
in a single word. It is to redeem himself, by his own efforts, from
this paradox that Faustus turns longing eyes on the magic books
that will make him 'a mighty god' – and ultimately damn him for
ever.

Dr Faustus is a tragedy of damnation. In his source Marlowe
found the story of a scholar who gave his soul to the devil in return
for twenty-four years of knowledge and pleasure. The rewards were
miserably inadequate, and are shown as such in the play, where
Faustus is seen as a spectator at a conventional masque of the Seven
Deadly Sins; as an astronaut circling the world; as a common
illusionist entertaining at a Royal Command performance; and as a
mystical greengrocer contenting a pregnant duchess with out-of-
season grapes. Some critics, like Warren D. Smith, claim that the
trivialities of the middle parts of the play show Marlowe intent on
'establishing evil, though terrible in consequence, as actually petty
in nature'.[3] On such a reading one can trace a gradual deterioration
in the character of the protagonist:

> From a proud philosopher, master of all human knowledge, to a trickster,
> to a slave of phantoms, to a cowering wretch: that is a brief sketch of the
> progress of Dr Faustus.[4]

Robert Ornstein, however, sees no such deterioration in Dr Faustus,

[1] J. B. Steane, *Marlowe* (1965), p. 141
[2] *Essays*, 'Of Cunning'
[3] 'The Nature of Evil in *Dr Faustus*', *M.L.R.*, LX (April, 1965), p. 171
[4] Helen Gardner, 'The Tragedy of Damnation', *Elizabethan Drama*, ed. R. J.
Kaufmann (New York, 1961), p. 321

arguing that the scholar 'grows more gracious'[1] as he approaches his catastrophe; and Clifford Leech finds that

> Faustus's moment of highest authority, the moment when he is nearest to freedom, is not when he signs the bond but when he addresses the shape of Helen and puts himself into hell.[2]

Perhaps every critic creates his *own* Faustus, interpreting 'Dr Faustus' – both the play and its eponymous hero – according to his personal experience and philosophy!

Even so, the interpretation must be based on an attempt to understand Marlowe's position, and some of the ideas which he shared with the Elizabethan audiences – whose approval of the play is vouched by the box-office receipts recorded in Henslowe's *Diary*.

Quarrelsome, violent, homosexual, a mocking atheist – this is the Marlowe of contemporary scandal, and the one who is best known today. But before this came the holder of the Archbishop Parker scholarship, the Cambridge student of divinity who – from the evidence of this last play – studied the theological texts in the library of Corpus Christi as avidly and earnestly as his Faustus promises to read Lucifer's presentation volume. Evidence of this is in Mephastophilis' account of the torments of deprivation:

> Think'st thou that I, who saw the face of God,
> And tasted the eternal joys of heaven,
> Am not tormented with ten thousand hells
> In being deprived of everlasting bliss!
>
> Scene 3, lines 78–81

The notion is not that of *EFB*, nor does it come from Marlowe's own imagination: the words are directly translated from the Latin of St John Chrysostom (see note p. 20). Just before this Faustus, refusing to distinguish between the Christian hell and the pagan Elysium, proposes for himself an eternity among the Greek philosophers in the words of Averroes (see note p. 19). Marlowe the theologian has at least as great a part in this play as Marlowe the rebel.

Faustus takes his first step along the primrose path when he sets material benefits before spiritual blessings. Contemplating magic, anticipating its rewards with Valdes and Cornelius, he promises himself all the glory and riches of the Renaissance world. From Mephastophilis he demands to 'live in all voluptuousness' (Scene 3, line 93). Even before he succumbs to the lure of magic, his mind has been tempted by thoughts of wealth: 'Be a physician, Faustus, heap

---

[1] Robert Ornstein, 'Marlowe and God: The Tragic Theology of *Dr Faustus*', *PMLA*, LXXXIII (1968)

[2] Clifford Leech, *Christopher Marlowe: Poet for the Stage* (New York, 1986), p. 98

up gold' (Scene 1, line 14). Yet although this obsession with luxury is a flaw in the nature of one dedicated to the search for knowledge, its seriousness must not be magnified until it obscures the real issues. In the first soliloquy Faustus rejects the study of law, leaving it to the 'mercenary drudge Who aims at nothing but external trash' (Scene 1, lines 34–5); all the gold that the doctor can heap up will not reconcile him to the limitations of medical skill, through whose aid he can restore only health, not life.[1] And when, in an early agony of indecision, he weighs the profit and the loss, it is not riches that he puts into the opposite scale:

> Have not I made blind Homer sing to me
> Of Alexander's love, and Oenon's death?
> And hath not he that built the walls of Thebes
> With ravishing sound of his melodious harp,
> Made music with my Mephastophilis?
>
> Scene 5, lines 202–6

With the help of magic he has gained entry into another world, later to be represented in the form of Helen of Troy, whose value far exceeds the riches of all the Venetian argosies, Indian gold, and Orient pearl.

The process of damnation begins with the signing of the pact. Greg[2] was the first critic to take serious notice of the first article in the infernal contract: 'that Faustus may be a spirit in form and substance' (Scene 5, line 96). To the Elizabethans, *spirit* used in this way could mean only 'devil', and by assuming diabolic nature Faustus, in the eyes of the orthodox, would be instantly damned. Lucifer and all the fallen angels were beyond the reach of God's mercy; although God still had power to forgive, they lacked the capacity to repent and *receive* forgiveness. Aquinas is the chief authority here, and his doctrine, expounded in *Summa Theologica* i, 64, is echoed to the letter in one of Donne's sermons:

> To those that fell, can appertain no reconciliation; no more then to those that die in their sins; for *Quod homini mors, Angelis casus*; The fall of the Angels wrought upon them, as the death of a man does upon him.
>
> *LXXX Sermons* (1640), p. 9

To Lucifer, with his legalistic turn of mind, the contract is binding:

> Christ cannot save thy soul, for he is just.
> There's none but I have interest in the same.
>
> Scene 5, lines 259–60

---

[1] Christopher Ricks discusses the importance of the medical skill in a plague-ridden England in '*Doctor Faustus* and Hell on Earth', *E & S*, XXXV, No. 2 (April, 1985), pp. 101–120

[2] 'The Damnation of Faustus', *M.L.R.*, XLI (1946)

The Evil Angel is similarly insistent, telling Faustus flatly

> Thou art a spirit, God cannot pity thee.
>
> Scene 5, line 189

The play would have stopped at this point, so far as the tragic part is concerned, had Faustus, the Good Angel, and Marlowe himself shared Lucifer's opinion as to the irrevocability of the compact. But there is still hope in the Good Angel's comforting words: 'Faustus repent, yet God will pity thee' (Scene 5, line 188). By signing the bond with its ominous first clause Faustus is not cut off from forgiveness; but the effects of his sin, in turning away from God, make it virtually impossible for him to accept the offered mercy. Repentance is all that is needed, yet to his dismay he finds 'My heart's so hardened I cannot repent' (Scene 5, line 194).

The devils are adept at pricking the bubble of human self-glorification, and Faustus' pride is punctured in his first encounter with Mephastophilis. Soaring, as he thinks, to the height of his powers as 'conjuror laureate', he is jolted sharply back to earth by the fiend's casual admission that the conjuring was of no real import: 'I came now hither of mine own accord' (Scene 3, line 45). Hell's rewards are as the Dead Sea apples to Milton's fallen angels: mere ashes in his mouth. Repeated questioning of Mephastophilis brings no satisfaction; the devil can tell him only what he already knows and, forbidden to speak the praise of God, cannot give him the answer he wants to hear:

> FAUSTUS   Tell me who made the world?
> MEPHASTOPHILIS
>   I will not.
>
> Scene 5, lines 241–2

His pride dashed, Faustus becomes increasingly aware of the emptiness of his bargain and the reality of damnation. The pride with which this Renaissance superman scorned his human nature and aspired to become 'a mighty god' leads him inevitably to its opposite, despair; and from this there is no salvation.

There are some sins on which God will have no mercy; although He will forgive violation of the decalogue, and even blasphemy against Christ, yet

> whosoever speaketh against the Holy Ghost, it shall not be forgiven him, neither in this world, neither in the world to come.
>
> Matthew xii, 32

The precise nature of the sin against the Holy Ghost, not defined in the Gospel, has always exercised theologians; but Renaissance thinkers generally agreed that pride and despair, inextricably linked, must be so called. The 'Schoolemen', writes Donne, have noted certain sins

> which they have called sins against the Holy Ghost, because naturally they shut out those meanes by which the Holy Ghost might work upon us. The first couple is, *presumption* and *desperation*; for presumption takes away the fear of God, and desperation the love of God . . . And truly . . . To presume upon God, that God cannot damn me eternally in the next world, for a few half-houres in this . . . Or to despair, that God will not save me . . . al these are shrewd and slippery approaches towards the sin against the Holy Ghost.
>
> *LXXX Sermons*, pp. 349–50

The play ends where it began, in the solitude of Faustus' study, and it is here that Faustus finally damns himself, although for a moment, just after the Old Man's speech, he comes very close to repentance and salvation.

The Old Man comes, like the personification of Mercy in the Morality Play *Mankind* who rescues the protagonist from worldly snares, to advise Faustus that there is still a chance that he will be saved from eternal damnation. The man who has abjured the Scriptures, forsaken God, and trafficked with the devil, can still implore

> mercy, Faustus, of thy saviour sweet,
> Whose blood alone must wash away thy guilt.
>
> Scene 12, lines 36–7

But hell's present physical tortures terrify him more than the thought of future damnation, and instead of withstanding the momentary agony (as the Old Man will do later) Faustus requests instead the comfort of

> That heavenly Helen which I saw of late,
> Whose sweet embracings may extinguish clean
> These thoughts that do dissuade me from my vow.
>
> Scene 12, lines 75–7

Helen of Troy, twice passing over the stage, pausing for one brief moment yet speaking nothing, is the key figure in *Dr Faustus*. For this, Faustus has sold his soul. All the glory that was Greece was embodied, for the Renaissance, in this woman; her story was the story in brief of another world, superhuman and immortal. Helen's first appearance to the Scholars is no accident, no mere matter of a dramatist making double use of a bright idea. After their single appearance (Scene 2) at the beginning of the play the Scholars seem to have been forgotten; but this scene has shown them to be men of moderate awareness, eminently sensible and a little humourless. Their comments on the apparition (Scene 12, lines 16–24) equip us to judge for ourselves when it is seen again. Helen is the 'only paragon of excellence' in the eyes of these sober men, and their ordinary understanding is 'Too simple ... to tell her praise'. The second appearance, attended by two Cupids and heralded, we must assume, by the music directed for the earlier entrance, has a ritual solemnity. This, and the formal ordering of Faustus' speech, mark the episode as what T. S. Eliot would have called 'a moment in and out of time'.[1] Faustus breaks the silence with the awed amazement of some of Marlowe's finest lines:

> Was this the face that launched a thousand ships,
> And burnt the topless towers of Ilium?
>
> Scene 12, lines 81–2

Declaring his devotion, he is exalted to heroic stature and promises vigorous action in verse of soaring energy which comes to rest at last on Helen's lips:

> And then return to Helen for a kiss.
>
> Scene 12, line 93

The speech is a rapture of applause – for Helen herself, for the eternal beauty of form, for all the glory that defies and withstands the canker of Time. But it is more than this. As the delighted verse surges forward to praise what is lovely and enduring, an undertow drags back to remind us that this beauty brought destruction: a city was burnt, topless towers laid in the dust. In the stillness of a single couplet the two movements are balanced:

> Brighter art thou than flaming Jupiter
> When he appeared to hapless Semele.
>
> Scene 12, lines 96–7

Semele, despite repeated warnings, persisted in her demands to see her lover in all his splendour. But the sight of Jupiter's divine majesty was greater than mortal eyes could bear to look upon, and the 'hapless Semele' was consumed by the glory. Helen has all of Jupiter's terrible burning beauty – and Faustus is damned by the vision. This is no mere fancy of Marlowe's, powerful though such a fancy would be. That which appears as Helen is no more the woman herself than the apparition which so pleased the German emperor was indeed Alexander. Faustus sees a spirit, a devil, in the form of Helen and, forgetful of his admonitions to the emperor, he speaks to it and touches it. Helen's lips 'suck forth' his soul in more than metaphor. The kiss signals the ultimate sin, demoniality, the bodily

---

[1] *Four Quartets*, 'Little Gidding'

intercourse with spirits.[1] Now the Old Man gives up hope of saving Faustus. After such knowledge there is no forgiveness.

The last soliloquy reverses the first. The proud scholar who had fretted at the restrictions imposed by the human condition and longed for the immortality of a god now seeks to avoid an eternity of damnation. Like a trapped animal he lashes out against the mesh he has woven for himself, and becomes more entangled. To be physically absorbed, to be 'a creature wanting soul', 'some brutish beast', even, at the last, to be no more than 'little water drops' – this is the final hope of the pride of Wittenberg. Time is the dominant in this speech. The measured regularity of the opening gives way to a frantic tugging in two directions as Faustus suffers the opposing forces of Christ and Lucifer:

> O I'll leap up to my God! Who pulls me down?
>
> Scene 13, line 71

The pace and the passion increase as the clock strikes relentlessly, and the second half-hour passes more quickly than the first. We are agonizingly aware of the last minutes of Faustus' life, trickling through the hour-glass with what seems like ever-increasing speed. But as each grain falls, bringing Faustus closer to his terrible end, we become more and more conscious of the deserts of vast eternity and damnation that open up beyond death. When Macbeth or Lear dies the tragedy is ended with a final harmonious chord, but the discords of Faustus' last lines cannot be easily resolved.

Dr Faustus has much in common with the late medieval Morality Plays; but there is much that is different. The eponymous heroes of *Mankind* and *Everyman* are, like Faustus, tempted to sin; and they fall. But, counselled by the representations of Mercy and Knowledge, they recognize the error of their ways, repent, and are redeemed. Faustus, however, finding his heart 'so hardened [he] cannot repent', is in a worse dilemma than his predecessors – perhaps because he is more intelligent and individual than them. John Donne's Sonnet IV articulates the problem:

> Yet grace, if thou repent, thou canst not lack;
> But who shall give thee that grace, to begin?

Marlowe's sympathies (if the energy of the verse means anything at all) are for the rebel, who is impeded in his pursuit of science and frustrated in his efforts to assert his individuality. But he also feels deeply for the bleakly unhappy Mephastophilis, who is possessed of all the knowledge that Faustus desires, and who is 'tormented with ten thousand hells' because he has forfeited the 'everlasting bliss' that the doctor is so ready to part with.

---

[1] First pointed out by Greg in the essay referred to above

FURTHER READING

Bevington, David — *From 'Mankind' to Marlowe* (Harvard, 1962)

Bowers, Fredson — 'Marlow's *Dr Faustus*: the 1602 Additions', *Studies in Bibliography* 26 (1973)

Brockbank, J. P. — *Marlowe: 'Dr Faustus'* (1962)

Cole, Douglas — *Suffering and Evil in the Plays of Christopher Marlowe* (1964)

Empson, William — *Faustus and the Censor: The English Faustbook and Marlowe's 'Dr. Faustus'* ed. John Henry Jones (Oxford: Blackwell, 1987)

Gardber, Helen — 'The Tragedy of Damnation', *Elizabethan Drama*, ed. R. J. Kaufmann (New York, 1961)

Greg, W. W. — 'The Damnation of Faustus', *M.L.R.*, XLI (1946)

Hotson, Leslie — *The Death of Christopher Marlowe* (1925)

Jump, John (ed.) — *Marlowe: 'Dr Faustus' – a casebook* (1969)

Leech, Clifford — *Christopher Marlowe: poet for the stage* (New York, 1986)

Levin, Harry — *The Overreacher* (1954)

Mangan, Michael — *'Doctor Faustus': A Critical Study* (Harmondsworth: Penguin Books, 1987)

Pettitt, T. — 'The Folk-Play in Marlowe's *Dr Faustus*', *Folklore* 9:1 (1980)

Ricks, Christopher — *'Dr Faustus* and Hell on Earth', *Essays in Criticism*, XXXV, No. 3 (April; 1985)

Sales, Roger — *Christopher Marlowe* (Houndmills, Basingstoke and London: Macmillan, 1991)

Sanders, Wilbur — *The Dramatist and the Received Idea* (1968)

Steane, J. B. — *Marlowe: a critical study* (1964)

Two editions present A and B texts together

Greg, W. W. (ed.) — *Marlowe's 'Dr Faustus' 1604-1616; Parallel Texts* (Oxford: Clarendon Press, 1950)

Bevington, D. and Rasmussen, E. — *Dr Faustus*, Revels Plays (Manchester: Manchester University Press, 1993)

THE
TRAGICALL
History of D. Fauſtus.

As it hath bene Acted by the Right
Honorable the Earle of Nottingham his ſeruants.

Written by Ch. Marl.

LONDON
Printed by V.S, for Thomas Buſhell. 1604.

The printer's device on the titlepage is McKerrow 142; it is described as 'A boy with wings upon his right arm and with his left hand holding, or fastened to, a weight', the emblem signifying talent frustrated by poverty. It was not unique to *Dr Faustus*: the printer, Simmes, had used it on several other books, including the 1597 quarto of Shakespeare's *Richard II*

(Photo: Bodleian Library, Oxford)

[DRAMATIS PERSONAE

Chorus

Dr John Faustus
Wagner *his servant, a student*
Valdes ⎱ *his friends, magicians*
Cornelius ⎰
Three Scholars

The Good Angel
The Evil Angel
Mephastophilis
Lucifer
Belzebub
Old Man

The Clown
Robin ⎱ *ostlers at an inn*
Rafe ⎰
Vintner
Horse-courser

The Pope
The Cardinal of Lorraine

The Emperor Charles V
A Knight *at the emperor's court*
Duke of Vanholt
Duchess of Vanholt

(list continued overleaf)

Mephastophilis This version of the character's name is used consistently
throughout the A Text; the B Text spelling, 'Mephostophilis', is used in the
Appendix of scenes from that text. William Empson has a note on the various
spellings in *Faustus and the Censor* (1987), pp. 45–6*n*

Spirits presenting
The Seven Deadly Sins
                Pride
                Covetousness
                Wrath
                Envy
                Gluttony
                Sloth
                Lechery
Alexander the Great and his Paramour
Helen of Troy

Attendants, Friars, and Devils]

DR FAUSTUS

Prologue

Enter CHORUS

CHORUS

Not marching now in fields of Thrasimene,
Where Mars did mate the Carthaginians,
Nor sporting in the dalliance of love,
In courts of kings where state is overturned,
Nor in the pomp of proud audacious deeds,   5
Intends our Muse to vaunt his heavenly verse:
Only this (Gentlemen) we must perform,
The form of Faustus' fortunes good or bad.
To patient judgements we appeal our plaud,
And speak for Faustus in his infancy: 10
Now is he born, his parents base of stock,
In Germany, within a town called Rhodes;
Of riper years to Wittenberg he went,
Whereas his kinsmen chiefly brought him up.
So soon he profits in divinity,   15

---

s.d. *Chorus* Marlowe uses a single figure (subsequently identified with Wagner) to introduce the play and link the dramatic episodes; the 'Chorus' here fulfils the function of the 'Doctor' or presenter, of the Morality Plays

1–5 The Prologue speaks of plays already performed, but – whether these were written by Marlowe or merely part of the company's repertoire – the references are unclear. There is no trace of any play showing the victory of the Carthaginians under Hannibal at Lake Thrasymenus in 217 B.C.; and any number of plays (including Marlowe's own *Edward II*) could be said to show 'the dalliance of love' in royal courts

2 *Mars* the Roman god of war
 mate ally himself with

3 *dalliance* frivolity

6 *our Muse* our poet; the Chorus is speaking on behalf of the acting company
 vaunt B (daunt A) show off

9 *appeal our plaud* ask for applause

12 *Rhodes* Roda, since 1922 Stadtroda (in East Germany)

13 *Wittenberg* Hamlet's university, and Luther's, was the home of scepticism; but this Wittenberg is, in all outward appearances, Marlowe's own Cambridge

14 *Whereas* where

The fruitfull plot of scholarism graced,
That shortly he was graced with doctor's name,
Excelling all, whose sweet delight disputes
In heavenly matters of theology.
Till, swollen with cunning, of a self conceit,   20
His waxen wings did mount above his reach,
And melting heavens conspired his overthrow.
For falling to a devilish exercise,
And glutted more with learning's golden gifts,
He surfeits upon cursed necromancy: 25
Nothing so sweet as magic is to him,
Which he prefers before his chiefest bliss.
And this the man that in his study sits.

                                                    Exit

Scene 1

Enter FAUSTUS *in his Study*

FAUSTUS
Settle thy studies, Faustus, and begin
To sound the depth of that thou wilt profess:
Having commenced, be a divine in show,
Yet level at the end of every art,
And live and die in Aristotle's works.   5

16 a credit to the rich discipline of academic studies
17 *graced* At Cambridge, an official 'grace' permits a candidate to proceed to his
   degree; Marlowe's name is entered in the Grace Book for 1584 and 1587
18 *whose sweet delight disputes* whose great pleasure is in academic debate
20 *cunning* knowledge; usually knowledge misapplied
   self conceit pride in his own abilities
21 *waxen wings* In Greek mythology, Icarus flew too near the sun on wings of wax;
   they melted, and he fell into the sea. The fall of Icarus became a popular
   Renaissance emblem throughout Europe
27 *chiefest bliss* i.e. hope of life after death
28 *this the man* This seems to be the cue for the Chorus to draw aside a curtain and
   disclose Faustus in his study
 2 *sound* measure
   profess specialize in, study and teach
 3 *commenced* graduated; a Cambridge term
   divine theologian
   in show in appearance
 4 consider the purpose of every discipline
5–37 In his survey of human scholarship Faustus resembles the protagonist of
   Lyly's *Euphues* (1578) who determines to return to the university:
       Philosophie, Phisicke, Divinitie, shal be my studie. O yᵉ hidden secrets of
       Nature, the expresse image of morall vertues, the equall ballaunce of Justice,

Sweet *Analytics*, 'tis thou hast ravished me:
Bene disserere est finis logices.
Is, to dispute well, logic's chiefest end?
Affords this art no greater miracle?
Then read no more, thou hast attained the end;   10
A greater subject fitteth Faustus' wit.
Bid *on kai me on* farewell; Galen come:
Seeing, *ubi desinit philosophus, ibi incipit medicus.*
Be a physician, Faustus, heap up gold,
And be eternized for some wondrous cure.   15
Summum bonum medicinae sanitas:
The end of physic is our body's health.
Why Faustus, hast thou not attained that end?
Is not thy common talk found aphorisms?
Are not thy bills hung up as monuments,   20

---

the medicines to heale all diseases, how they beginne to delyght me. The
Axiomaes of *Aristotle*, the *Maxims* of *Justinian*, the *Aphorismes* of *Galen*,
have sodaynelye made such a breache into my minde, that I seem onely to
desire them which did onely earst detest them.

Euphues, ed. Bond (1902), i.241

5–7 Aristotle had been the dominant figure in the university curriculum since the
thirteenth century, but in Marlowe's day his supremacy was challenged by the
intellectual reformer Petrus Ramus. *Analytics* is the name given to two of
Aristotle's works on the nature of proof in argument, but the definition of logic
in line 7 comes in fact from Ramus' *Dialecticae*. Ramus, his ideas, and his
violent death are displayed in Marlowe's *Massacre at Paris*

12 *on kai me on* being and not being. A1 prints a jumble of letters, 'Oncaymaeon',
which later editions, trying to make some sense out of them, changed to
'Oeconomy'. Bullen recognized A's apparent gibberish as a transliteration of the
Greek phrase, from a work attributed to the philosopher Georgias of Leontini
(*c.* 483–376 B.C.)

Galen A second-century Greek physician who was accepted as an authority on
medical science throughout the Middle Ages

13 since the doctor starts where the philosopher leaves off; Aristotle, *de sensu*, ch 1,
436a

14 *heap up gold* The association of gold and the medical profession is an old one;
Shakespeare mentions the use of gold for 'Preserving life in med'cine potable'
(*2 Henry IV*, IV, v, 162). Faustus, however, is thinking of the profit to be
gained – like Chaucer's Physician in *The Canterbury Tales*:

For gold in phisik is a cordial,
Therefore he lovede gold in special.   (Prologue, 444–5)

15 *eternized* immortalized

16 Aristotle, *Nicomachean Ethics*, 1094. a. 8; Faustus translates in line 17

19 Faustus ranks himself with Hippocrates, whose *Aphorismes* was the most
famous of medical textbooks

found B (sound A) thought to be

20 *bills* prescriptions

Whereby whole cities have escaped the plague,
And thousand desperate maladies been eased?
Yet art thou still but Faustus, and a man.
Couldst thou make men to live eternally,
Or, being dead, raise them to life again,   25
Then this profession were to be esteemed.
Physic farewell! Where is Justinian?
Si una eademque res legatur duobus,
Alter rem alter valorem rei, etc.
A pretty case of paltry legacies: 30
Exhereditare filium non potest pater nisi . . .
Such is the subject of the Institute,
And universal body of the law:
This study fits a mercenary drudge
Who aims at nothing but external trash!   35
Too servile and illiberal for me.
When all is done, divinity is best:
Jerome's Bible, Faustus, view it well:
Stipendium peccati mors est: ha! *Stipendium, etc.*
The reward of sin is death? That's hard.   40
Si peccasse negamus, fallimur, et nulla est in nobis veritas.
If we say that we have no sin,
We deceive ourselves, and there's no truth in us.
Why then belike we must sin,
And so consequently die.   45

21 *Whereby* i.e. through the efficacy of the drugs
24 *Could'st . . . men* B (Would'st . . . man A); B's emendation is justifiable on
     grounds of common sense: Faustus longs for the divine power to grant eternal
     life, or the power of Christ (who raised Lazarus from the dead: St John i. 1–44)
27 Justinian was a Roman emperor of the sixth century A.D., who re-organized the
     whole of Roman Law in his *Corpus Juris* ('Body of the Law'); the first part,
     Institutiones, was a manual intended for law-students
28–9 'If one and the same thing is bequeathed to two persons, one should have the
     thing itself, the other the value of the thing': Justinian, *Institutes*, ii. 20
31 'A father cannot disinherit his son unless . . .': Justinian, ii. 13
33 *law* B (church A)
34 *This study* B (His study A)
36 *Too servile* B (The devil A)
     illiberal Faustus compares the mercenary concerns of the lawyers with the
     culturally enriching studies of the 'liberal arts'
38 *Jerome's Bible* the Vulgate, prepared mainly by St Jerome; but the texts that
     Faustus quotes are not in the Latin of the Vulgate
39 Romans vi, 23; but Faustus reads only half of the verse
41 I John i, 8. By again reading only half the verse, Faustus fails to register the
     offered comfort: 'If we confess our sins, he is faithful and just to forgive us our
     sins, and to cleanse us from all unrighteousness'

Ay, we must die an everlasting death.
What doctrine call you this? *Che sara, sara*:
What will be, shall be! Divinity, adieu!
These metaphysics of magicians,
And necromantic books are heavenly!   50
Lines, circles, schemes, letters and characters!
Ay, these are those that Faustus most desires.
O what a world of profit and delight,
Of power, of honour, of omnipotence
Is promised to the studious artisan!   55
All things that move between the quiet poles
Shall be at my command; emperors and kings
Are but obeyed in their several provinces,
Nor can they raise the wind, or rend the clouds;
But his dominion that exceeds in this   60
Stretcheth as far as doth the mind of man:
A sound magician is a mighty god.
Here Faustus, try thy brains to gain a deity.

Enter WAGNER

Wagner, commend me to my dearest friends,
The German Valdes, and Cornelius,   65
Request them earnestly to visit me.
WAGNER
I will sir.   *Exit*
FAUSTUS
Their conference will be a greater help to me,
Than all my labours, plod I ne'er so fast.

Enter the GOOD ANGEL *and the* EVIL ANGEL

GOOD ANGEL
O Faustus, lay that damned book aside,   70
And gaze not on it, lest it tempt thy soul,
And heap God's heavy wrath upon thy head:
Read, read the Scriptures; that is blasphemy.

47 'What will be, shall be'
51 *schemes* Gill (scenes A; *om* B); diagrams
55 *artisan* craftsman
56 *quiet poles* the poles of the universe, quiet because unmoving
58 *several* respective
60 *exceeds* excels
   this i.e. this magic art

EVIL ANGEL
Go forward, Faustus, in that famous art,
Wherein all nature's treasury is contained: 75
Be thou on earth as Jove is in the sky,
Lord and commander of these elements.

Exeunt

FAUSTUS
How am I glutted with conceit of this!
Shall I make spirits fetch me what I please,
Resolve me of all ambiguities,   80
Perform what desperate enterprise I will?
I'll have them fly to India for gold,
Ransack the ocean for orient pearl,
And search all corners of the new found world
For pleasant fruits and princely delicates.   85
I'll have them read me strange philosophy,
And tell the secrets of all foreign kings;
I'll have them wall all Germany with brass,
And make swift Rhine circle fair Wittenberg;
I'll have them fill the public schools with silk,   90
Wherewith the students shall be bravely clad.
I'll levy soldiers with the coin they bring,
And chase the Prince of Parma from our land,

76 *Jove* The names of the pagan deities were frequently attributed to the Christian God; there is special force in this coming from the Evil Angel
77 *these elements* the four elements – earth, air, fire, and water – of which the world was made
78 *glutted with conceit* drunk with the thought
80 *Resolve me of* give me the answers to
ambiguities problems
81 *desperate* daring
83 *orient pearl* The most precious pearls were from the Indian Ocean
84 *new found* newly discovered
85 *delicates* delicacies
86 *read me* teach me
88 *wall ... brass* Friar Bacon, in Greene's *Friar Bacon and Friar Bungay* (before 1592) intended to 'circle England round with brass' (ii. 29) when his magic schemes reached fruition
89 *swift Rhine* Wittenberg in fact stands on the river Elbe
90 *public schools* university lecturerooms
silk Dyce (skill Qq (all quartos)); in Marlowe's day, undergraduates were ordered to dress soberly
91 *bravely* smartly
93–6 The Prince of Parma was Spanish governor-general of the United Provinces of the Netherlands, 1579–92; he had earlier been responsible for building a bridge across the Scheldt (in the blockade of Antwerp), which was attacked and destroyed by a fire-ship in April 1589

And reign sole king of all our provinces.
Yea, stranger engines for the brunt of war,   95
Than was the fiery keel at Antwerp's bridge,
I'll make my servile spirits to invent.
Come German Valdes and Cornelius,
And make me blest with your sage conference.

Enter VALDES *and* CORNELIUS

Valdes, sweet Valdes, and Cornelius,   100
Know that your words have won me at the last
To practise magic and concealed arts;
Yet not your words only, but mine own fantasy,
That will receive no object for my head,
But ruminates on necromantic skill.   105
Philosophy is odious and obscure,
Both law and physic are for petty wits;
Divinity is basest of the three,
Unpleasant, harsh, contemptible and vile.
'Tis magic, magic that hath ravished me.   110
Then, gentle friends, aid me in this attempt,
And I, that have with concise syllogisms
Gravelled the pastors of the German church,
And made the flowering pride of Wittenberg
Swarm to my problems, as the infernal spirits   115
On sweet Musaeus when he came to hell,
Will be as cunning as Agrippa was,
Whose shadows made all Europe honour him.
VALDES
Faustus, these books, thy wit, and our experience
Shall make all nations to canonize us.   120
As Indian Moors obey their Spanish lords,

---

 95 *engines* machines   *brunt* assault
102 *concealed* occult
103 *fantasy* imagination
104 'Which won't let me think of anything else'
112 *concise syllogisms* clever arguments
113 *Gravelled* confounded
115 *problems* topics of academic debate
116 *Musaeus* Virgil (*Aeneid* vi, 667–8) describes this legendary, pre-Homeric bard
     (*not* the author of *Hero and Leander*) surrounded by the spirits of priests and
     bards in the Elysian fields of the Greek underworld
117 *Agrippa* The magician and necromancer Henry Cornelius Agrippa von
     Nettesheim (1486–1535) was famous for his reputed power of invoking shades
     of the dead
121 *Indian Moors* American Indians

So shall the spirits of every element
Be always serviceable to us three.
Like lions shall they guard us when we please,
Like Almaine rutters with their horsemen's staves,   125
Or Lapland giants trotting by our sides;
Sometimes like women, or unwedded maids,
Shadowing more beauty in their airy brows
Than in the white breasts of the Queen of Love.
From Venice shall they drag huge argosies,   130
And from America the golden fleece
That yearly stuffs old Philip's treasury,
If learned Faustus will be resolute.

FAUSTUS
Valdes, as resolute am I in this
As thou to live, therefore object it not.   135

CORNELIUS
The miracles that magic will perform
Will make thee vow to study nothing else.
He that is grounded in astrology,
Enriched with tongues, well seen in minerals,
Hath all the principles magic doth require: 140
Then doubt not, Faustus, but to be renowned
And more frequented for this mystery,
Than heretofore the Delphian oracle.

122 *spirits* B (subjects A); A's reading seems to be a mistaken attempt by the
     compositor to carry on the sense of the preceding line; the 'spirits' are the
     elemental genii
125 'Like German cavalry with lances'
126 *Lapland giants* On another occasion Marlowe refers to the inhabitants of the
     polar regions in this way: 'tall and sturdy men, Giants as big as hugy
     Polypheme' (*2 Tamburlaine*, I, i, 37–8)
129 *in the* Greg (in their A; has the B)
130 *From* A2 (For A1)
     argosies treasureships
131–2 America, whose richness is compared to the golden fleece sought by Jason and
     the Argonauts, paid annual tribute to Philip of Spain; 'stuffs' became 'stuffed' in
     the B Text, in recognition of the death of Philip II
135 *object it not* don't raise any objections
138 *grounded* well schooled
139 *tongues* Greek and Hebrew were desirable for those who would converse with
     spirits, but Latin was the recognized common language: 'Thou art a scholar:
     speak to it Horatio.' *Hamlet*, I, i, 42
     seen in minerals B (seen minerals A); knowledgeable about the properties of
     minerals
142 'More sought after for practising this art'
143 *Delphian oracle* the oracle of Apollo at Delphi

The spirits tell me they can dry the sea,
And fetch the treasure of all foreign wrecks,   145
Ay, all the wealth that our forefathers hid
Within the massy entrails of the earth.
Then tell me, Faustus, what shall we three want?

FAUSTUS
Nothing Cornelius! O this cheers my soul!
Come, show me some demonstrations magical,   150
That I may conjure in some lusty grove,
And have these joys in full possession.

VALDES
Then haste thee to some solitary grove,
And bear wise Bacon's and Abanus' works,
The Hebrew Psalter, and New Testament;   155
And whatsoever else is requisite
We will inform thee ere our conference cease.

CORNELIUS
Valdes, first let him know the words of art,
And then, all other ceremonies learned,
Faustus may try his cunning by himself.   160

VALDES
First, I'll instruct thee in the rudiments,
And then wilt thou be perfecter than I.

FAUSTUS
Then come and dine with me, and after meat
We'll canvass every quiddity thereof:
For ere I sleep, I'll try what I can do.   165
This night I'll conjure, though I die therefore.

Exeunt

---

147 *massy* solid
151 *lusty* A1 (little A2,3; bushy B); in the sixteenth century, the word could mean 'pleasant'
154 *wise Bacon's and Abanus' works* Roger Bacon (?1214–94), protagonist of Greene's *Friar Bacon and Friar Bungay*, was an Oxford philosopher popularly supposed to have dabbled in black magic. Abanus is perhaps Pietro d'Abano (?1250–1316), Italian humanist and physician, who was also believed to have been a conjuror. As well as the works of these two, which would supply formulae for incantation, Faustus would need certain Psalms (especially 22 and 51) and the opening words of St John's Gospel for his conjuring
161 *rudiments* 'all that which is called vulgarly the vertue of worde, herbe, & stone: which is used by unlawful charmes, without natural causes ... such kinde of charmes as commonlie daft wives use.' James I, *Daemonologie* (Edinburgh, 1597), p. 11
164 *canvass every quiddity* explore every detail; *quiddity* is a scholastic term denoting the essence of a thing, that which makes it what it is

Scene 2

Enter two SCHOLARS

1 SCHOLAR
I wonder what's become of Faustus, that was wont to make
our schools ring with *sic probo*.
2 SCHOLAR
That shall we know; for see, here comes his boy.

Enter WAGNER

1 SCHOLAR
How now sirra, where's thy master?
WAGNER
God in heaven knows.   5
2 SCHOLAR
Why, dost not thou know?
WAGNER
Yes I know, but that follows not.
1 SCHOLAR
Go to sirra, leave your jesting, and tell us where he is.
WAGNER
That follows not necessary by force of argument, that you,
being licentiates, should stand upon't; therefore acknow-   10
ledge your error, and be attentive.
2 SCHOLAR
Why, didst thou not say thou knew'st?
WAGNER
Have you any witness on't?
1 SCHOLAR
Yes sirra, I heard you.
WAGNER
Ask my fellow if I be a thief.   15
2 SCHOLAR
Well, you will not tell us.

---

  2 *sic probo* thus I prove it: a term from scholastic disputation
 10 *licentiates* graduates; holders of a degree permitting them to study for higher
     (master's or doctor's) degrees
     stand upon't understand
12–15 This seems to have been the formula for some kind of stock theatrical
     'business', drawing the audience into the comedy routine

WAGNER

Yes sir, I will tell you; yet if you were not dunces you
would never ask me such a question. For is not he *corpus
naturale*? And is not that *mobile*? Then wherefore should
you ask me such a question? But that I am by nature   20
phlegmatic, slow to wrath, and prone to lechery – to love I
would say – it were not for you to come within forty foot of
the place of execution, although I do not doubt to see you
both hanged the next sessions. Thus having triumphed over
you, I will set my countenance like a precisian, and begin to   25
speak thus: Truly my dear brethren, my master is within at
dinner with Valdes and Cornelius, as this wine, if it could
speak, it would inform your worships. And so the Lord
bless you, preserve you, and keep you, my dear brethren,
my dear brethren.   30

Exit

1 SCHOLAR
Nay then, I fear he is fallen into that damned art, for which
they two are infamous through the world.
2 SCHOLAR
Were he a stranger, and not allied to me, yet should I grieve
for him. But come, let us go and inform the Rector, and see
if he by his grave counsel can reclaim him.   35
1 SCHOLAR
Ay, but I fear me nothing can reclaim him.
2 SCHOLAR
Yet let us try what we can do.

Exeunt

17 *dunces* blockheads. The followers of Duns Scotus were commonly known as
   Dunses, but here it is Wagner himself who indulges in the academic cavilling
   characteristic of the Scotists
18–19 *corpus . . . mobile* a natural body and [therefore] capable of movement:
   Aristotle's *corpus naturale seu mobile* was the current scholastic definition of the
   subject-matter of physics
23 *place of execution* i.e. the dining-room; Wagner continues to make comic capital
   out of the phrase
25 *precisian* puritan; Wagner now apes the unctuous speech of this sect
34 *Rector* head of the university

Scene 3

Enter FAUSTUS *to conjure*

FAUSTUS

Now that the gloomy shadow of the earth,
Longing to view Orion's drizzling look,
Leaps from th'antarctic world unto the sky,
And dims the welkin with her pitchy breath:
Faustus, begin thine incantations,   *calls*   5
And try if devils will obey thy hest,
Seeing thou hast prayed and sacrificed to them.
Within this circle is Jehovah's name,   *the*
Forward and backward anagrammatized;   *devils*
Th'abbreviated names of holy saints,   10
Figures of every adjunct to the heavens,
And characters of signs and erring stars,
By which the spirits are enforced to rise.
Then fear not Faustus, but be resolute,
And try the uttermost magic can perform.   15
Sint mihi dei acherontis propitii. Valeat numen triplex

1 *shadow of the earth* In *The French Academie*, La Primaudaye explains that 'the
   night, also, is no other thing than the shadow of the earth'. Cf. also John Norton
   Smith, 'Marlowe's *Faustus*', *N & Q* NS 25 (1978), pp. 436–7
2 *Orion's drizzling look* the rainy constellation of Orion
3 Marlowe seems to have thought that night advances from the southern
   hemisphere
7 *prayed and sacrificed* A period of prayer and sacrifice, a kind of spiritual
   preparation, was a pre-requisite for conjuring
8–13 Before he began his conjuring, the magician would draw a circle round
   himself, inscribing on the periphery certain signs (of the zodiac, for instance)
   and the tetragrammaton, the four Hebrew letters of the Divine Name. This was
   not only part of the invocation: so long as the circle was unbroken and the
   magician stayed inside it, no evil spirit could harm him
9 *anagrammatized* B (and agramathist A)
10 *Th'abbreviated* B (The breviated A)
11 *adjunct* heavenly body joined to the firmament (see note on Scene 5, lines
   211–19)
12 *characters* symbols
   signs i.e. of the zodiac
   erring stars planets
16–23 'May the gods of Acheron look favourably upon me. Away with the spirit of
   the three-fold Jehovah. Welcome, spirits of fire, air, water, and earth. We ask
   your favour, O Prince of the East, Belzebub, the monarch of burning hell, and
   Demogorgon, that Mephastophilis may appear and rise. Why do you delay? By

Jehovae! Ignei, aerii, terreni, aquatici spiritus salvete!
Orientis princeps, Belzebub inferni ardentis monarcha, et
Demogorgon, propitiamus vos, ut appareat et surgat Meph-
astophilis. Quid tu moraris? Per Jehovam, Gehennam, et   20
consecratam aquam quam nunc spargo; signumque crucis
quod nunc facio; et per vota nostra, ipse nunc surgat nobis
dicatus Mephastophilis.

Enter a DEVIL

I charge thee to return and change thy shape,
Thou art too ugly to attend on me;   25
Go and return an old Franciscan friar,
That holy shape becomes a devil best.   *Exit* DEVIL
I see there's virtue in my heavenly words!
Who would not be proficient in this art?

Jehovah, Gehenna, and the holy water which I now sprinkle, and the sign of the
cross which I now form, and by our vows, may Mephastophilis himself now rise,
compelled to obey us.'

Rejecting the God of Heaven, the Christian God in Three Persons, Faustus
turns to His infernal counterpart: Acheron is one of the rivers in the Greek
underworld, the Prince of the East is Lucifer (see Isaiah xiv, 12), and
Demogorgon is, in classical mythology, one of the most terrible primeval gods.
Faustus hails the spirits of the elements: 'they make them believe, that at the fall
of *Lucifer*, some spirits fell in the aire, some in the fire, some in the water, some
in the lande' (*Daemonologie*, p. 20). The name of Mephastophilis was not,
apparently, known before the Faust legend; this seems to have been Marlowe's
preferred spelling – it is the one used most frequently in the A Text. The
different spellings are discussed by William Empson in *Faustus and the Censor*,
1987.

Many invocations to the devil express similar surprise and impatience at his
delay, after which the conjuror redoubles his efforts. Gehenna, the valley of
Hinnom, was a place of sacrifice. Dr Faustus seems now to be renouncing his
Christian baptism, misusing the baptismal water and forswearing the vows
made at his christening. In devil-worship, the sign of the cross had a double
function: a powerful charm to overcome diabolic disobedience, it also protected
the conjuror from injury by any spirit that might appear

17 *terreni* Greg (*om* Qq); Faustus would invoke the spirits of all four elements
18 *Belzebub* Marlowe's form of the name has been retained because at certain
points (e.g. Scene 5, line 12) this suits better with the metre than the more
commonly used Hebraic Beelzebub
20 *Quid tu moraris* Ellis (*quod tumeraris* Qq)
24 *change thy shape EFB* describes a creature of fire, which appears at this point
and eventually takes the shape of a man; the B Text asks for a 'Dragon' in what
seems to be an anticipatory stage direction, and the woodcut on the B titlepage
shows an emergent dragon on the ground beside the conjuror's circle. A wary
magician always stipulated from the beginning that a pleasing shape should be
assumed

How pliant is this Mephastophilis, 30
Full of obedience and humility,
Such is the force of magic and my spells.
Now Faustus, thou art conjuror laureate
That canst command great Mephastophilis.
Quin redis, Mephastophilis, fratris imagine! 35

Enter MEPHASTOPHILIS

MEPHASTOPHILIS
Now Faustus, what would'st thou have me do?
FAUSTUS
I charge thee wait upon me whilst I live,
To do what ever Faustus shall command,
Be it to make the moon drop from her sphere,
Or the ocean to overwhelm the world. 40
MEPHASTOPHILIS
I am a servant to great Lucifer,
And may not follow thee without his leave;
No more than he commands must we perform.
FAUSTUS
Did not he charge thee to appear to me?
MEPHASTOPHILIS
No, I came now hither of mine own accord. 45
FAUSTUS
Did not my conjuring speeches raise thee? Speak!
MEPHASTOPHILIS
That was the cause, but yet *per accidens*,
For when we hear one rack the name of God,
Abjure the Scriptures, and his saviour Christ,
We fly in hope to get his glorious soul, 50
Nor will we come, unless he use such means
Whereby he is in danger to be damned:
Therefore the shortest cut for conjuring
Is stoutly to abjure the Trinity,
And pray devoutly to the prince of hell. 55

33 *laureate* The laurel wreath of excellence was given to poets in ancient Greece
35 'Why do you not return, Mephastophilis, in the likeness of a friar'
  redis Boas (*regis* A; this line, and the two preceding ones, are omitted in B)
39–40 Faustus would share these powers with the enchanters of classical literature
  (see Kocher, p. 141)
45 What Kocher (p. 160) calls the 'doctrine of voluntary ascent' is fairly well
  established in witchcraft
47 *per accidens* only in appearance; what the conjuring represented was the real
  cause
48 *rack* violate: 'take the name of the Lord in vain'

FAUSTUS

   So Faustus hath already done, and holds this principle:

   There is no chief but only Belzebub,

   To whom Faustus doth dedicate himself.

   This word damnation terrifies not him,

   For he confounds hell in Elysium: 60

   His ghost be with the old philosophers.

   But leaving these vain trifles of men's souls,

   Tell me, what is that Lucifer thy lord?

MEPHASTOPHILIS

   Arch-regent and commander of all spirits.

FAUSTUS

   Was not that Lucifer an angel once?   65

MEPHASTOPHILIS

   Yes Faustus, and most dearly loved of God.

FAUSTUS

   How comes it then that he is prince of devils?

MEPHASTOPHILIS

   O, by aspiring pride and insolence,

   For which God threw him from the face of heaven.

FAUSTUS

   And what are you that live with Lucifer?   70

MEPHASTOPHILIS

   Unhappy spirits that fell with Lucifer,

   Conspired against our God with Lucifer,

   And are for ever damned with Lucifer.

FAUSTUS

   Where are you damned?

MEPHASTOPHILIS

   In hell.   75

FAUSTUS

   How comes it then that thou art out of hell?

---

60 *confounds hell in Elysium* makes no distinction between the Christian concept
   of hell and the pagan (Greek) notion of the after-life in Elysium. Marlowe has
   already coupled the two: 'Hell and Elysium swarm with ghosts of men' (*1
   Tamburlaine*, V,ii, 403). Nashe may be referring to either of these passages
   when he scorns the writers that 'thrust Elisium into hell' (Preface to Greene's
   Menaphon [1589], ed. McKerrow, iii, 316)

61 *old philosophers* those who shared his disbelief in an eternity of punishment; the
   line seems to come from a saying of Averroes: *sit anima mea cum philosophis*
   (cf. J. C. Maxwell, *N & Q*, CXIV [1949], pp. 334–5; J. M. Steadman, *N & Q*,
   CCVII [1962], pp. 327–9)

63 *that Lucifer* A simple account of the history of Lucifer is given in Isaiah xiv,
   12–15

MEPHASTOPHILIS

Why this is hell, nor am I out of it.
Think'st thou that I, who saw the face of God,
And tasted the eternal joys of heaven,
Am not tormented with ten thousand hells   80
In being deprived of everlasting bliss!
O Faustus, leave these frivolous demands,
Which strike a terror to my fainting soul.

FAUSTUS

What, is great Mephastophilis so passionate
For being deprived of the joys of heaven?   85
Learn thou of Faustus manly fortitude,
And scorn those joys thou never shalt possess.
Go bear these tidings to great Lucifer,
Seeing Faustus hath incurred eternal death
By desperate thoughts against Jove's deity: 90
Say, he surrenders up to him his soul
So he will spare him four and twenty years,
Letting him live in all voluptuousness,
Having thee ever to attend on me,
To give me whatsoever I shall ask,   95
To tell me whatsoever I demand,
To slay mine enemies, and aid my friends,
And always be obedient to my will.
Go, and return to mighty Lucifer,
And meet me in my study at midnight,   100
And then resolve me of thy master's mind.

MEPHASTOPHILIS

I will Faustus.   *Exit*

[Marginal annotations, handwritten:]
Hell in right here – anywhere that God is not.
F. does not know what it is to lose God.
devil defines himself in relation to God
7. can't hear the terror
surrenders his soul
too Lucifer
although M. told him not to.
F. has Pride autonomy from God, like L.

77–81 Caxton, while locating hell 'in the most lowest place, most derke, and most vyle of the erthe', stressed that it is a state as well as a place; the condemned sinner is like a man 'that had a grete maladye, so moche that he sholde deye, and that he were brought into a fair place and plesaunt for to have Joye and solace; of so moche shold he be more hevy and sorowful' (*The Mirrour of the World* [1480], ii, 18). Marlowe's concept of hell at this point may be compared with Milton's; like Mephastophilis, Satan cannot escape:

> For within him Hell
> He brings, and round about him, nor from Hell
> One step, no more than from himself can fly
> By change of place.   *Paradise Lost*, iv, 20–23

Mephastophilis' account of the torment of deprivation is translated from St John Chrysostom: *si decem mille gehennas quis dixerit, nihil tale est quale ab illa beata visione excidere* (see John Searle, *T.L.S.*, 15 February 1936)
88 *these* B (those A)
92 *So* on condition that

FAUSTUS
  Had I as many souls as there be stars
  I'd give them all for Mephastophilis.
  By him I'll be great emperor of the world,   *Power*   105
  And make a bridge through the moving air
  To pass the ocean with a band of men;
  I'll join the hills that bind the Afric shore,
  And make that land continent to Spain,
  And both contributory to my crown.   110
  The emperor shall not live but by my leave,
  Nor any potentate of Germany.
  Now that I have obtained what I desire
  I'll live in speculation of this art
  Till Mephastophilis return again.   115

                                                                 Exit

Scene 4

Enter WAGNER *and the* CLOWN   *comic interludes*

WAGNER
  Sirra boy, come hither.
CLOWN
  How, boy? Zounds, boy! I hope you have seen many boys
  with such pickadevants as I have. Boy, quotha!
WAGNER
  Tell me sirra, hast thou any comings in?
CLOWN
  Ay, and goings out too; you may see else.   5
WAGNER
  Alas poor slave, see how poverty jesteth in his nakedness!
  The villain is bare, and out of service, and so hungry, that I
  know he would give his soul to the devil for a shoulder of
  mutton, though it were blood raw.

106-7 Faustus plans to emulate Xerxes, who built a bridge (using boats) across the
      Hellespont for his army to march over
108-9 The hills on either side of the Straits of Gibraltar would, if joined together,
      unite Africa and Europe into a single continent
Scene 4 The B Text version of this scene, which is greatly changed to accommodate
      different comedians and an altered theatrical taste, is printed in the Appendix
  3 *pickadevants* small, pointed beards
  4 *comings in* earnings, income
  5 *goings out* expenses; but the Clown makes the word serve two purposes,
      pointing also to his tattered clothing
  7 *out of service* out of a job

CLOWN

    How, my soul to the devil for a shoulder of mutton though   10
    'twere blood raw? Not so good friend; by'rlady, I had need
    have it well roasted, and good sauce to it, if I pay so dear.

WAGNER

    Well, wilt thou serve me, and I'll make thee go like *qui mihi*
    discipulus?

CLOWN

    How, in verse?   15

WAGNER

    No sirra; in beaten silk and stavesacre.

CLOWN

    How, how, knavesacre? Ay, I thought that was all the land
    his father left him! Do ye hear, I would be sorry to rob you
    of your living.

WAGNER

    Sirra, I say in stavesacre.   20

CLOWN

    Oho, oho, stavesacre! Why then belike, if I were your man,
    I should be full of vermin.

WAGNER

    So thou shalt, whether thou be'st with me or no. But sirra,
    leave your jesting, and bind your self presently unto me for
    seven years, or I'll turn all the lice about thee into familiars,   25
    and they shall tear thee in pieces.

CLOWN

    Do you hear sir? You may save that labour: they are too
    familiar with me already – zounds, they are as bold with my
    flesh as if they had paid for my meat and drink.

WAGNER

    Well, do you hear sirra? Hold, take these guilders.   30

CLOWN

    Gridirons; what be they?

13–14 *qui mihi discipulus* you who are my pupil: the opening words of a didactic
     Latin poem by the schoolmaster William Lily which would be familiar to every
     Elizabethan schoolboy

16 *beaten silk and stavesacre* 'In effect Wagner promises to dress his servant (or
     rather to dress him down) in silk – and adds that plenty of Keating's powder will
     be needed' (Greg). Gold or silver was hammered into silk as a kind of
     embroidery; *stavesacre* was a preparation from delphinium seeds used for killing
     fleas

17 *knavesacre* The Clown is fond of this kind of word-play, which was outdated by
     the time of Shakespeare's *Two Gentlemen of Verona* (*c.* 1594–5) where Speed
     shows a weary tolerance of Launce's jesting: 'Well, your old vice still: mistake
     the word' (III,i, 285)

WAGNER
Why, French crowns.
CLOWN
'Mass, but for the name of French crowns a man were as good
have as many English counters! And what should I do with these?
WAGNER
Why, now, sirra, thou art at an hour's warning whensoever   35
or wheresoever the devil shall fetch thee.
CLOWN
No, no, here take your gridirons again.
WAGNER
Truly I'll none of them.
CLOWN
Truly but you shall.
WAGNER
Bear witness I gave them him.   40
CLOWN
Bear witness I give them you again.
WAGNER
Well, I will cause two devils presently to fetch thee away.
Baliol and Belcher!
CLOWN
Let your Baliol and your Belcher come here, and I'll knock
them, they were never so knocked since they were devils!   45
Say I should kill one of them, what would folks say? Do ye

---

32 French crowns, legal tender in England in the 16th and early 17th centuries,
   were easily counterfeited. Marlowe himself is reported in the Baines libel as
   having boasted 'That he had as good Right to Coine as the Queen of England
   and that . . . he ment, through the help of a Cunninge stamp maker to Coin
   ffrench Crownes pistoletes and English shillinges'. Among government
   measures to stop the flood of false coins was a proclamation of 1587 urging all
   who were offered such pieces to strike a hole in them (see Ruding, *Annals of the
   Coinage of Britain* [1817], i, 192ff); perhaps the Clown refers to such mutilation
   when he describes Wagner's coins as *gridirons*
33 *'Mass* by the holy mass
34 *counters* worthless tokens
38–42 The business with the coins must be similar to that in scene viii of *The
   Taming of A Shrew* where the Clown starts a sequence with 'Here, here, take
   your two shillings again'. The actors draw the audience into their comic play to
   'Bear witness'
43 *Baliol* probably a corruption of 'Belial'; *Belcher* is also perhaps a mispronunciation of 'Belzebub'
44 *knock* beat
46–8 A similar passage occurs in *A Looking Glass for London* which was written by
   Lodge and Greene, acted by Strange's Men in 1592, and printed in 1594. Here

see yonder tall fellow in the round slop, he has killed the
devil! So I should be called 'Killdevil' all the parish over.

Enter two DEVILS, *and the* CLOWN *runs up
and down crying*

WAGNER
Baliol and Belcher, spirits, away!

Exeunt [DEVILS]

CLOWN
What, are they gone? A vengeance on them! They have vile   50
long nails. There was a he devil and a she devil. I'll tell you
how you shall know them: all he devils has horns, and all
she devils has clefts and cloven feet.

WAGNER
Well sirra, follow me.

CLOWN
But do you hear? If I should serve you, would you teach me   55
to raise up Banios and Belcheos?

WAGNER
I will teach thee to turn thy self to anything, to a dog, or a
cat, or a mouse, or a rat, or any thing.

CLOWN
How! A Christian fellow to a dog, or a cat, a mouse, or a
rat? No, no sir, if you turn me into anything, let it be in the   60
likeness of a little pretty frisking flea, that I may be here,
and there, and everywhere. O I'll tickle the pretty wenches'
plackets! I'll be amongst them i'faith.

WAGNER
Well sirra, come.

CLOWN
But, do you hear Wagner . . . ?   65

WAGNER
Baliol and Belcher!

---

the Clown attacks the devil who has come to carry him to hell; when the devil
pleads that he is mortally wounded, the Clown triumphs:
  Then may I count my selfe I thinke a tall man, that am able to kill a diuell.
  Now who dare deale with me in the parish, or what wench in *Ninivie* will not
  loue me, when they say, there goes he that beate the diuell.

(G3ᵛ)

47 *tall* fine
   round slop baggy pants
53 *clefts* slits
61 *frisking flea* In the medieval 'Song of the Flea', the poet envies the flea because
   it has free access to all parts of his mistress's body

CLOWN

O Lord I pray sir, let Banio and Belcher go sleep.

WAGNER

Villain, call me Master Wagner; and let thy left eye be
diametarily fixed upon my right heel, with *quasi vestigias
nostras insistere.*　　　　　　　　　　　　　　　　70

Exit

CLOWN

God forgive me, he speaks Dutch fustian! Well, I'll follow
him, I'll serve him; that's flat.

Exit

[handwritten: a new servant will be Fautus / his servant Wagner called devils & stares / fear in him]

Scene 5

Enter FAUSTUS *in his Study*

FAUSTUS

Now Faustus, must thou needs be damned,
And canst thou not be saved.
What boots it then to think of God or heaven?
Away with such vain fancies and despair,
Despair in God, and trust in Belzebub.
Now go not backward: no, Faustus, be resolute;
Why waverest thou? O, something soundeth in mine ears:
'Abjure this magic, turn to God again'.
Ay, and Faustus will turn to God again.
To God? He loves thee not:　　　　　　　　　　10
The god thou servest is thine own appetite
Wherein is fixed the love of Belzebub.
To him I'll build an altar and a church,
And offer luke-warm blood of new-born babes.

[handwritten margin notes: 2 beings... traditional – medieval (schizophrenia); turning as going back to God but will not; Selfish – desires define who he is; ↓ New identity is located in his reason.]

Enter GOOD ANGEL *and* EVIL [ANGEL]

GOOD ANGEL

Sweet Faustus, leave that execrable art.

FAUSTUS　　　　　　　　　　　　　　　　　　15

Contrition, prayer, repentance: what of them?

69 *diametarily* diametrically
69–70 *quasi vestigias nostras insistere* as it were tread in our footsteps; the
　　construction is false (for *vestigiis nostris*), but this may be intentional
71 *Dutch fustian* gibberish – double Dutch; *fustian* is a coarse cloth made of flax
　　and cotton

GOOD ANGEL
  O they are means to bring thee unto heaven.
EVIL ANGEL
  Rather illusions, fruits of lunacy,   → pray & repentance
  That makes men foolish that do trust them most.
GOOD ANGEL
  Sweet Faustus, think of heaven, and heavenly things.   20
EVIL ANGEL
  No Faustus, think of honour and of wealth.

            Exeunt [ANGELS]

FAUSTUS
  Of wealth!
  Why, the signory of Emden shall be mine
  When Mephastophilis shall stand by me.
  What god can hurt thee, Faustus? Thou art safe,   25
  Cast no more doubts. Come Mephastophilis,
  And bring glad tidings from great Lucifer.
  Is't not midnight? Come Mephastophilis:
  Veni, veni Mephastophile.

     Enter MEPHASTOPHILIS

  Now tell me, what says Lucifer thy lord?   30
MEPHASTOPHILIS
  That I shall wait on Faustus whilst he lives,
  So he will buy my service with his soul.
FAUSTUS
  Already Faustus hath hazarded that for thee.
MEPHASTOPHILIS
  But Faustus, thou must bequeath it solemnly,
  And write a deed of gift with thine own blood,   35
  For that security craves great Lucifer.
  If thou deny it, I will back to hell.
FAUSTUS
  Stay Mephastophilis, and tell me,
  What good will my soul do thy lord?

---

21 *and of wealth* A2 (and wealth A1)
23 *signory of Emden* governorship of Emden – a port on the mouth of the Ems, at
 this time trading extensively with England
29 'Come, O come Mephastophilis'
30 *tell me what* B (tell what A)
31 *he lives* B (I live A)
32 *So* provided that
33 *hazarded* jeopardized

MEPHASTOPHILIS
  Enlarge his kingdom.   40
FAUSTUS
  Is that the reason he tempts us thus?
MEPHASTOPHILIS
  Solamen miseris socios habuisse doloris.
FAUSTUS
  Have you any pain that torture others?
MEPHASTOPHILIS
  As great as have the human souls of men.
  But tell me Faustus, shall I have thy soul?   45
  And I will be thy slave and wait on thee,
  And give thee more than thou hast wit to ask.
FAUSTUS
  Ay Mephastophilis, I give it thee.
MEPHASTOPHILIS
  Then stab thine arm courageously,
  And bind thy soul, that at some certain day   50
  Great Lucifer may claim it as his own,
  And then be thou as great as Lucifer.
FAUSTUS
  Lo Mephastophilis, for love of thee,
  I cut mine arm, and with my proper blood
  Assure my soul to be great Lucifer's,   55
  Chief lord and regent of perpetual night.
  View here the blood that trickles from mine arm,
  And let it be propitious for my wish.
MEPHASTOPHILIS
  But Faustus, thou must write it
  In manner of a deed of gift.   60
FAUSTUS
  Ay, so I will; but Mephastophilis,
  My blood congeals and I can write no more.
MEPHASTOPHILIS
  I'll fetch thee fire to dissolve it straight.

Exit

40 *Enlarge his kingdom* 'Satan's chiefest drift & main point that he aimeth at, is the inlargement of his own kingdom, by the eternall destruction of man in the life to come', James Mason, *The Anatomie of Sorcerie* (1612), p. 55
42 In Chaucer's version: 'Men seyn, "to wrecche is consolacioun To have an-other felawe in his peyne".' *Troilus and Criseyde*, i, 708–9
43 *torture* B (tortures A)
54 *proper* own
58 *propitious* an acceptable sacrifice – as the blood of Christ is a propitiation for the sins of mankind

FAUSTUS

What might the staying of my blood portend?
Is it unwilling I should write this bill?   65
Why streams it not, that I may write afresh:
'Faustus gives to thee his soul': ah, there it stayed!
Why should'st thou not? Is not thy soul thine own?
Then write again: 'Faustus gives to thee his soul'.

Enter MEPHASTOPHILIS *with a chafer of coals*

MEPHASTOPHILIS

Here's fire, come Faustus, set it on.   70

FAUSTUS

So, now the blood begins to clear again.
Now will I make an end immediately.

MEPHASTOPHILIS

O what will not I do to obtain his soul!

FAUSTUS

Consummatum est, this bill is ended,
And Faustus hath bequeathed his soul to Lucifer.   75
But what is this inscription on mine arm?
Homo fuge. Whither should I fly?
If unto God, he'll throw thee down to hell;
My senses are deceived, here's nothing writ;
I see it plain, here in this place is writ,   80
Homo fuge! Yet shall not Faustus fly.

MEPHASTOPHILIS

I'll fetch him somewhat to delight his mind.

                                                                   Exit

Enter [again] with DEVILS, *giving crowns and rich
apparel to* FAUSTUS; *they dance, and then depart*

FAUSTUS

Speak Mephastophilis, what means this show?

MEPHASTOPHILIS

Nothing Faustus, but to delight thy mind withal,
And to show thee what magic can perform.   85

FAUSTUS

But may I raise up spirits when I please?

69 s.d. *chafer* portable grate
70 *set it on* 'set his blood in a saucer on warm ashes' *EFB*, vi
71 Greg observes that no earthly fire will liquefy congealed blood
74 *Consummatum est* It is completed; the last words of Christ on the cross: St John
   xix, 30
77 *Homo fuge* Fly, O man

MEPHASTOPHILIS
  Ay Faustus, and do greater things than these.
FAUSTUS
  Then there's enough for a thousand souls!
  Here Mephastophilis, receive this scroll,
  A deed of gift of body and of soul: 90
  But yet conditionally, that thou perform
  All articles prescribed between us both.
MEPHASTOPHILIS
  Faustus, I swear by hell and Lucifer
  To effect all promises between us made.
FAUSTUS
  Then hear me read them. On these conditions following: 95
  First, that Faustus may be a spirit in form and substance.
  Secondly, that Mephastophilis shall be his servant, and at his
  command.
  Thirdly, that Mephastophilis shall do for him, and bring him
  whatsoever.   100
  Fourthly, that he shall be in his chamber or house invisible.
  Lastly, that he shall appear to the said John Faustus at all
  times, in what form or shape soever he please.
  I, John Faustus of Wittenberg, doctor, by these presents, do
  give both body and soul to Lucifer, Prince of the East, and 105
  his minister Mephastophilis; and furthermore grant unto
  them that, four and twenty years being expired, the articles
  above written inviolate, full power to fetch or carry the said
  John Faustus, body and soul, flesh, blood, or goods, into their
  habitation wheresoever.   110
                             By me John Faustus.
MEPHASTOPHILIS
  Speak Faustus, do you deliver this as your deed?
FAUSTUS
  Ay, take it; and the devil give thee good on't.
MEPHASTOPHILIS
  Now Faustus, ask what thou wilt.
FAUSTUS
  First will I question with thee about hell: 115
  Tell me, where is the place that men call hell?
MEPHASTOPHILIS
  Under the heavens.

96 *a spirit* A spirit, to the Elizabethans, was usually an evil one – a devil (see
    Shakespeare, Sonnet CXLIV); according to some theologians, who followed
    Aquinas, God could have no mercy on a devil who was *ipso facto* incapable of
    repenting. See lines 189–91
104 *these presents* the legal articles

FAUSTUS
   Ay, but whereabouts?
MEPHASTOPHILIS
   Within the bowels of these elements,
   Where we are tortured and remain for ever.   120
   Hell hath no limits, nor is circumscribed
   In one self place; for where we are is hell,
   And where hell is, must we ever be.
   And to conclude, when all the world dissolves,
   And every creature shall be purified,   125
   All places shall be hell that is not heaven.
FAUSTUS
   Come, I think hell's a fable.
MEPHASTOPHILIS
   Ay, think so still, till experience change thy mind.
FAUSTUS
   Why? think'st thou then that Faustus shall be damned?
MEPHASTOPHILIS
   Ay, of necessity, for here's the scroll   130
   Wherein thou hast given thy soul to Lucifer.
FAUSTUS
   Ay, and body too; but what of that?
   Thinkest thou that Faustus is so fond to imagine
   That after this life there is any pain?
   Tush, these are trifles and mere old wives' tales.   135
MEPHASTOPHILIS
   But Faustus, I am an instance to prove the contrary;
   For I am damned, and am now in hell.
FAUSTUS
   How, now in hell? Nay, and this be hell, I'll willingly be
   damned here! What, walking, disputing, etc ... But leaving
   off this, let me have a wife, the fairest maid in Germany, for I 140
   am wanton and lascivious, and cannot live without a wife.
MEPHASTOPHILIS
   How, a wife? I prithee Faustus, talk not of a wife.
FAUSTUS
   Nay sweet Mephastophilis, fetch me one, for I will have one.

---

119 *these elements* the four elements (fire, air, earth, and water) below the sphere of
    the moon
122 *one self place* one particular place
133 *fond* foolish
138ff The writing here seems to degenerate as the text becomes merely an excuse
    for some stage business with the devil-wife
139 *disputing* According to the Prologue (line 18) this is Faustus's great delight

MEPHASTOPHILIS

    Well, thou wilt have one; sit there till I come.
    I'll fetch thee a wife in the devil's name.   145

                                       Exit

Enter [again] with a DEVIL *dressed like a woman,*
with fireworks

MEPHASTOPHILIS

    Tell Faustus, how dost thou like thy wife?

FAUSTUS

    A plague on her for a hot whore!

MEPHASTOPHILIS

    Tut Faustus, marriage is but a ceremonial toy;
    If thou lovest me, think no more of it.
    I'll cull thee out the fairest courtesans,   150
    And bring them every morning to thy bed:
    She whom thine eye shall like, thy heart shall have,
    Be she as chaste as was Penelope,
    As wise as Saba, or as beautiful
    As was bright Lucifer before his fall.   155
    Hold, take this book, peruse it thoroughly:
    The iterating of these lines brings gold;
    The framing of this circle on the ground
    Brings whirlwinds, tempests, thunder and lightning.
    Pronounce this thrice devoutly to thy self,   160
    And men in armour shall appear to thee,
    Ready to execute what thou desirest.

FAUSTUS

    Thanks Mephastophilis, yet fain would I have a book
    wherein I might behold all spells and incantations, that I
    might raise up spirits when I please.   165

MEPHASTOPHILIS

    Here they are in this book.   *There turn to them*

FAUSTUS

    Now would I have a book where I might see all characters
    and planets of the heavens, that I might know their motions
    and dispositions.

148 *ceremonial toy* trifling ceremony
149 *think no more* B (think more A)
150 *cull* pick
153 *Penelope* wife of Ulysses, renowned for her fidelity to an absent husband
154 *Saba* the Queen of Sheba, who confronted Solomon with 'hard questions',
    1 Kings x
168 *motions* movements
169 *dispositions* situations

MEPHASTOPHILIS
   Here they are too.   *Turn to them* 170

FAUSTUS
   Nay, let me have one book more, and then I have done,
   wherein I might see all plants, herbs and trees that grow
   upon the earth.

MEPHASTOPHILIS
   Here they be.

FAUSTUS
   O thou art deceived!   175

MEPHASTOPHILIS
   Tut, I warrant thee.   *Turn to them*

FAUSTUS
   When I behold the heavens, then I repent,
   And curse thee, wicked Mephastophilis,
   Because thou hast deprived me of those joys.

MEPHASTOPHILIS
   Why Faustus,   180
   Think'st thou that heaven is such a glorious thing?
   I tell thee 'tis not half so fair as thou,
   Or any man that breathes on earth.

FAUSTUS
   How prov'st thou that?

MEPHASTOPHILIS
   It was made for man, therefore is man more excellent. 185

FAUSTUS
   If it were made for man, 'twas made for me:
   I will renounce this magic, and repent.

            Enter GOOD ANGEL *and* EVIL ANGEL

GOOD ANGEL
   Faustus repent, yet God will pity thee.

EVIL ANGEL
   Thou art a spirit, God cannot pity thee.

FAUSTUS
   Who buzzeth in mine ears I am a spirit?   190
   Be I a devil, yet God may pity me.
   Ay, God will pity me if I repent.

EVIL ANGEL
   Ay, but Faustus never shall repent.

                       Exeunt [ANGELS]

---

190 *buzzeth* whispers
191 *Be I* This could mean either 'Even if I am', or else 'Even though I were'

FAUSTUS
My heart's so hardened I cannot repent!
Scarce can I name salvation, faith, or heaven,   195
But fearful echoes thunders in mine ears,
'Faustus, thou art damned'; then swords and knives,
Poison, guns, halters, and envenomed steel,
Are laid before me to dispatch myself:
And long ere this I should have slain myself,   200
Had not sweet pleasure conquered deep despair.
Have not I made blind Homer sing to me
Of Alexander's love, and Oenon's death?
And hath not he that built the walls of Thebes
With ravishing sound of his melodious harp,   205
Made music with my Mephastophilis?
Why should I die then, or basely despair?
I am resolved! Faustus shall ne'er repent.
Come Mephastophilis, let us dispute again,
And argue of divine astrology.   210

194 Hardness (also called blindness) of heart is recognized as a very complex
    spiritual condition; the Litany of the Book of Common Prayer offers a special
    supplication: 'From all blindness of heart . . . Good Lord, deliver us'
198 *halters* hangman's ropes
202 *blind Homer* The Greek poet was traditionally held to be blind
203 *Alexander . . . death* Alexander (Homer's name for Paris, son of Priam) fell in
    love with Oenone before he encountered Helen. After he was wounded in the
    Trojan War, he was carried to Oenone and died at her feet, whereupon she
    stabbed herself
204–5 At the sound of Amphion's harp the stones were so affected that they rose of
    their own accord to form the walls of Thebes
210–39 The Faustus of Marlowe's source was an astrologer – a calendar-maker and
    weather-forecaster – rather than an astronomer; and although the spirit
    promises to teach him about the planets, his approach is unscientific and the
    information a miscellaneous jumble. Marlowe's protagonist has the questioning
    mind of the Renaissance student, and the answers he is given accord with the
    sceptical authorities of the day (see Kocher, pp. 214–23, and F. R. Johnson,
    'Marlowe's Astronomy and Renaissance Skepticism', *E.L.H.*, XIII [1946], iv).
    The Ptolemaic system, as yet unshaken by Copernicus, held that the universe
    was composed of concentric spheres with the earth (*this centric earth*) as the
    innermost. Beyond the earth was the sphere of the Moon, and further out still
    the spheres of the six other *erring stars* or planets: Mercury, Venus, Sun, Mars,
    Jupiter, Saturn. The eighth was the firmament, or sphere of the fixed stars,
    which Marlowe, admitting only nine spheres (1. 235) identified with the
    Primum Mobile, the first moving thing which imparted movement to all the rest.
    The ninth sphere (tenth, if the *Primum Mobile* was allowed to be separate from
    the firmament) was the immovable empyrean (*the empyreal orb*)

Tell me, are there many heavens above the moon?
Are all celestial bodies but one globe,
As is the substance of this centric earth?

MEPHASTOPHILIS

As are the elements, such are the spheres,
Mutually folded in each other's orb.   215
And, Faustus, all jointly move upon one axletree
Whose termine is termed the world's wide pole,
Nor are the names of Saturn, Mars, or Jupiter,
Feigned, but are erring stars.

FAUSTUS

But tell me, have they all one motion, both *situ et*   220
tempore?

MEPHASTOPHILIS

All jointly move from east to west in four-and-twenty
hours upon the poles of the world, but differ in their
motion upon the poles of the zodiac.

FAUSTUS

Tush, these slender trifles Wagner can decide!   225
Hath Mephastophilis no greater skill?
Who knows not the double motion of the planets?
The first is finished in a natural day, the second thus: as
Saturn in thirty years; Jupiter in twelve; Mars in four; the
Sun, Venus, and Mercury in a year; the Moon in twenty-   230

211–19 *Tell me ... erring stars* Faustus asks first for confirmation of the number of
      spheres beyond the Moon, and whether in fact these do form a single ball.
      Mephastophilis replies that just as the four elements enclose each other (earth is
      surrounded by water, water by air, and air by fire), so each sphere or heaven is
      circled round by the ones beyond it, and all rotate upon a single axletree.
      Saturn, Mars, and the other planets are individually recognizable: they are
      called *erring* or wandering stars to distinguish them from the fixed stars which
      are joined to the firmament

217 *termine* boundary (astronomical)

220–31 *But ... days* 'Do all the planets move at the same speed and in the same
      direction?' is Faustus' next question. He is told that the planets have two
      movements: a daily west to east rotation round the earth governed by the
      Primum Mobile, and a slower, individual turning from west to east. Caxton
      (*Mirrour of the World* [1480], i, 13) explains that each planet is like a fly
      crawling on a wheel: if the fly crawls in one direction and the wheel turns in the
      opposite, the fly may be said to have two motions. Faustus knows this well
      enough, and proceeds to detail with reasonable accuracy the different times
      taken by the planets in their individual revolutions – the farthest from the earth,
      naturally, taking the longest. The figures usually given are: Saturn $29\frac{1}{2}$ years;
      Jupiter $11\frac{3}{4}$ years, Mars 1 year 11 months; Sun 1 year; Venus $7\frac{1}{2}$ months; and
      Mercury 3 months

220–1 *situ et tempore* in direction and time

eight days. Tush, these are freshmen's suppositions. But
tell me, hath every sphere a dominion or *intelligentia*?

MEPHASTOPHILIS

Ay.

FAUSTUS

How many heavens or spheres are there?

MEPHASTOPHILIS

Nine: the seven planets, the firmament, and the empyreal   235
heaven.

FAUSTUS

Well, resolve me in this question: why have we not
conjunctions, oppositions, aspects, eclipses, all at one time,
but in some years we have more, in some less?

231 *freshmen's suppositions* elementary facts given to first-year undergraduates for
them to build an argument upon

232 *hath ... intelligentia* The next question at issue relates to a theory first
propounded by Plato and developed in the Middle Ages, that each planet was
guided by an angelic spirit, commonly called the *intelligence*:

Let mans Soule be a Spheare, and then, in this,
The intelligence that moves, devotion is.
                    Donne, 'Good Friday, Riding Westwards'
Mephastophilis affirms the *intelligence*, but the theory was never really accepted
by scientists

234–6 *How many ... heaven* Faustus seems to return to his earlier query about the
number of spheres or heavens. Aristotle accounted for eight, but another was
added by the early Church Fathers who postulated the *empyreal heaven* which
was the abode of God, unmoving and shining with a piercing, stainless light.
Milton describes a similar cosmology in *Paradise Lost* when he identifies 'the
planets seven', 'the fixed', 'And that crystalline sphere ... that first moved' (III,
481–3)

237–40 *Resolve me ... totius* Mephastophilis' answer to the next question sounds
like a quotation from some astronomical textbook. Faustus asks about the
behaviour of the planets, using technical but well-known astronomical terms;
conjunctions are the apparent joinings together of two planets, whilst *oppositions*
describes their relationships when most remote:

Therefore the love which us doth bind,
But Fate so enviously debars,
Is the Conjunction of the Mind,
And Opposition of the Stars.
                    Marvell, 'The Definition of Love'
Any position between the two extremes of conjunction and opposition was
termed an *aspect*. To astrologers the differing situations and relations of the
planets all have some particular significance – hence the horoscope. Faustus is
finally told what he already knows: that the heavenly bodies do not all move at
the same speed, and that for this reason ('through an irregular motion so far as
the whole is concerned', 1. 240) there are more eclipses etc. in some years than
in others

MEPHASTOPHILIS
  Per inaequalem motum respectu totius.   240
FAUSTUS
  Well, I am answered. Tell me who made the world?
MEPHASTOPHILIS
  I will not.
FAUSTUS
  Sweet Mephastophilis, tell me.
MEPHASTOPHILIS
  Move me not, for I will not tell thee.
FAUSTUS
  Villain, have I not bound thee to tell me anything?   245
MEPHASTOPHILIS
  Ay, that is not against our kingdom; but this is.
  Think thou on hell Faustus, for thou art damned.
FAUSTUS
  Think, Faustus, upon God, that made the world.
MEPHASTOPHILIS
  Remember this.   *Exit*
FAUSTUS
  Ay, go accursed spirit, to ugly hell,   250
  'Tis thou hast damned distressed Faustus' soul:
  Is't not too late?

          Enter GOOD ANGEL *and* EVIL [ANGEL]

EVIL ANGEL
  Too late.
GOOD ANGEL
  Never too late, if Faustus can repent.
EVIL ANGEL
  If thou repent, devils shall tear thee in pieces.   255
GOOD ANGEL
  Repent, and they shall never rase thy skin.
                                    Exeunt [ANGELS]
FAUSTUS
  Ah Christ my Saviour, seek to save
  Distressed Faustus' soul.

          Enter LUCIFER, BELZEBUB *and* MEPHASTOPHILIS

244 *Move me not* Don't make me angry
256 *rase* graze

LUCIFER

Christ cannot save thy soul, for he is just.
There's none but I have interest in the same.   260

FAUSTUS

O who art thou that look'st so terrible?

LUCIFER

I am Lucifer, and this is my companion prince in hell.

FAUSTUS

O Faustus, they are come to fetch away thy soul!

LUCIFER

We come to tell thee thou dost injure us.
Thou talk'st of Christ, contrary to thy promise.   265
Thou should'st not think of God; think of the devil,
And of his dam too.

FAUSTUS

Nor will I henceforth: pardon me in this,
And Faustus vows never to look to heaven,
Never to name God, or to pray to him,   270
To burn his Scriptures, slay his ministers,
And make my spirits pull his churches down.

LUCIFER

Do so, and we will highly gratify thee. Faustus, we are
come from hell to show thee some pastime; sit down, and
thou shalt see all the Seven Deadly Sins appear in their   275
proper shapes.

FAUSTUS

That sight will be as pleasing unto me, as Paradise was to
Adam, the first day of his creation.

LUCIFER

Talk not of Paradise, nor creation, but mark this show; talk
of the devil and nothing else. Come away.   280

Enter the SEVEN DEADLY SINS

Now Faustus, examine them of their several names and
dispositions.

FAUSTUS

What art thou, the first?

PRIDE

I am Pride: I disdain to have any parents. I am like to
Ovid's flea, I can creep into every corner of a wench: 285

---

260 *have interest in* have a legal claim on
281 *several* different
285 *Ovid's flea* The poet of 'Song of the Flea' (probably medieval but attributed to
      Ovid) envies the flea for its freedom of movement over his mistress' body

sometimes like a periwig, I sit upon her brow; or like a fan
of feathers, I kiss her lips. Indeed I do – what do I not! But
fie, what a scent is here? I'll not speak another word, except
the ground were perfumed and covered with cloth of arras.

FAUSTUS

What are thou, the second?   290

COVETOUSNESS

I am Covetousness, begotten of an old churl in an old
leathern bag: and might I have my wish, I would desire that
this house, and all the people in it, were turned to gold, that
I might lock you up in my good chest. O my sweet gold!

FAUSTUS

What art thou, the third?   295

WRATH

I am Wrath. I had neither father nor mother: I leaped out of
a lion's mouth when I was scarce half an hour old, and ever
since I have run up and down the world, with this case of
rapiers, wounding myself when I had nobody to fight
withal. I was born in hell – and look to it, for some of you   300
shall be my father.

FAUSTUS

What art thou, the fourth?

ENVY

I am Envy, begotten of a chimney-sweeper, and an oyster-
wife. I cannot read, and therefore wish all books were
burnt; I am lean with seeing others eat – O that there   305
would come a famine through all the world, that all might
die, and I live alone; then thou should'st see how fat I
would be! But must thou sit and I stand? Come down, with
a vengeance.

FAUSTUS

Away, envious rascal! What art thou, the fifth?   310

GLUTTONY

Who, I sir? I am Gluttony. My parents are all dead, and the
devil a penny they have left me but a bare pension, and
that is thirty meals a day and ten bevers – a small trifle to
suffice nature. O, I come of a royal parentage: my
grandfather was a gammon of bacon, my grandmother a   315
hogshead of claret wine; my godfathers were these: Peter

289 *cloth of arras* tapestry, woven at Arras in Flanders and used to make wall-
    hangings
292 *leathern bag* the miser's purse   298 *case* pair
300 *some of you* Wrath addresses the audience
303–4 *begotten . . . wife* Envy is filthy, and stinks
313 *bevers* snacks

Pickled-Herring, and Martin Martlemas-Beef. O, but my
godmother! She was a jolly gentlewoman, and well-beloved
in every good town and city; her name was Mistress
Margery March-Beer. Now, Faustus, thou hast heard all   320
my progeny; wilt thou bid me to supper?

FAUSTUS

No, I'll see thee hanged; thou wilt eat up all my victuals.

GLUTTONY

Then the devil choke thee!

FAUSTUS

Choke thyself, Glutton. What art thou, the sixth?

SLOTH

I am Sloth; I was begotten on a sunny bank, where I have   325
lain ever since – and you have done me great injury to bring
me from thence. Let me be carried thither again by
Gluttony and Lechery. I'll not speak another word for a
king's ransom.

FAUSTUS

What are you Mistress Minx, the seventh and last?   330

LECHERY

Who, I, sir? I am one that loves an inch of raw mutton
better than an ell of fried stockfish; and the first letter of
my name begins with Lechery.

LUCIFER

Away! To hell, to hell!

Exeunt the [SEVEN DEADLY] SINS

Now Faustus, how dost thou like this?   335

FAUSTUS

O this feeds my soul.

LUCIFER

Tut Faustus, in hell is all manner of delight.

FAUSTUS

O might I see hell, and return again, how happy were I
then!

---

317 *Martlemas-Beef* Meat, salted to preserve it for winter, was hung up around
     Martinmas (11 November)
320 *March-Beer* a rich ale, made in March and left to mature for at least two years
321 *progeny* lineage (obsolete)
331–3 *I am one . . . Lechery* The words are rather obscure, but their sense is clear.
     Lechery prefers a small quantity of virility to a large extent of impotence:
     stockfish, a long strip of dried cod, is a common term of abuse, indicating
     impotence: 'he was begot between two stockfishes', *Measure for Measure*, III, ii,
     98. The 'Minx' ends with a common form of jest: cf. 'Her name begins with
     Mistress Purge', Middleton, *The Family of Love*, II, iii, 53

LUCIFER

Thou shalt; I will send for thee at midnight. In meantime,   340
take this book, peruse it thoroughly, and thou shalt turn
thyself into what shape thou wilt.

FAUSTUS

Great thanks, mighty Lucifer; this will I keep as chary as
my life.

LUCIFER

Farewell, Faustus; and think on the devil.   345

FAUSTUS

Farewell, great Lucifer; come Mephastophilis.

Exeunt omnes

Scene 6

Enter ROBIN *the ostler with a book in his hand*

ROBIN

O this is admirable! here I ha' stolen one of Doctor Faustus'
conjuring books, and i'faith I mean to search some circles
for my own use: now will I make all the maidens in our
parish dance at my pleasure stark naked before me, and so
by that means I shall see more than ere I felt, or saw yet.   5

Enter RAFE *calling* ROBIN

RAFE

Robin, prithee come away, there's a gentleman tarries to
have his horse, and he would have his things rubbed and
made clean. He keeps such a chafing with my mistress
about it, and she has sent me to look thee out. Prithee, come
away.   10

ROBIN

Keep out, keep out; or else you are blown up, you are

343 *chary* carefully
Scene 6 In the A Text the two episodes with Robin and Rafe are presented as a single
    scene following Chorus 3 – which is surely intended to introduce the scene at
    the papal court. This edition follows the B Text in its division and placing of the
    episodes, but the content of the scenes is that of the A Text; the Appendix prints
    B's version
  2 *circles* magicians' circles; but the sexual overtones are obvious
  8 *chafing* scolding

dismembered, Rafe. Keep out, for I am about a roaring
piece of work.

RAFE

Come, what dost thou with that same book? Thou canst not
read!   15

ROBIN

Yes, my master and mistress shall find that I can read – he
for his forehead, she for her private study. She's born to
bear with me, or else my art fails.

RAFE

Why Robin, what book is that?

ROBIN

What book? Why the most intolerable book for conjuring   20
that ere was invented by any brimstone devil.

RAFE

Canst thou conjure with it?

ROBIN

I can do all these things easily with it: first, I can make thee
drunk with 'ipocrase at any tavern in Europe for nothing,
that's one of my conjuring works.   25

RAFE

Our master parson says that's nothing.

ROBIN

True Rafe! And more, Rafe, if thou hast any mind to Nan
Spit, our kitchen-maid, then turn her and wind her to thy
own use, as often as thou wilt, and at midnight.

RAFE

O brave Robin! Shall I have Nan Spit, and to mine own   30
use? On that condition I'll feed thy devil with horsebread as
long as he lives, of free cost.

ROBIN

No more, sweet Rafe; let's go and make clean our boots
which lie foul upon our hands, and then to our conjuring in
the devil's name.   35

Exeunt

12 *roaring* dangerous
20 *intolerable* Robin probably means 'incomparable'
24 *'ipocrase* hippocras – a spiced wine
31 *horsebread* fodder for horses
32 *of free cost* free of charge

Chorus 2

Enter WAGNER *solus*

WAGNER
   Learned Faustus,
   To know the secrets of astronomy
   Graven in the book of Jove's high firmament,
   Did mount himself to scale Olympus' top,
   Being seated in a chariot burning bright,   5
   Drawn by the strength of yoked dragons' necks.
   He now is gone to prove cosmography,
   And, as I guess, will first arrive at Rome,
   To see the pope, and manner of his court,
   And take some part of holy Peter's feast,   10
   That to this day is highly solemnized.

Exit WAGNER

Scene 7

Enter FAUSTUS *and* MEPHASTOPHILIS

FAUSTUS
   Having now, my good Mephastophilis,
   Passed with delight the stately town of Trier,
   Environed round with airy mountain tops,
   With walls of flint, and deep entrenched lakes,
   Not to be won by any conquering prince;   5
   From Paris next, coasting the realm of France,
   We saw the river Main fall into Rhine,
   Whose banks are set with groves of fruitful vines;
   Then up to Naples, rich Campania,
   Whose buildings fair and gorgeous to the eye,   10

---

1 s.d. *Enter Wagner* This direction from the A Text suggests that all the choric
   speeches – including the Prologue and the Epilogue – were spoken by Wagner
4 *Olympus* Mount Olympus was the home of the gods of Greek mythology
6 *yoked* B (yoky A)
7 *cosmography* The B Text adds a line explaining that this 'measures costs, and
   kingdomes of the earth'
10 *holy Peter's feast* St Peter's feast day is 29 June
2 *Trier* Treves, in West Germany
9 *Campania* Naples lies within the region of Campania

The streets straight forth, and paved with finest brick,
Quarters the town in four equivalents;
There saw we learned Maro's golden tomb,
The way he cut, an English mile in length,
Thorough a rock of stone in one night's space.   15
From thence to Venice, Padua, and the rest,
In midst of which a sumptuous temple stands,
That threats the stars with her aspiring top.
Thus hitherto hath Faustus spent his time.
But tell me now, what resting place is this?   20
Hast thou, as erst I did command,
Conducted me within the walls of Rome?

MEPHASTOPHILIS
Faustus, I have; and because we will not be unprovided, I
have taken up his holiness' privy chamber for our use.

FAUSTUS
I hope his holiness will bid us welcome.   25

MEPHASTOPHILIS
Tut, 'tis no matter man, we'll be bold with his good cheer.
And now, my Faustus, that thou may'st perceive
What Rome containeth to delight thee with,
Know that this city stands upon seven hills
That underprop the groundwork of the same;   30
Just through the midst runs flowing Tiber's stream,
With winding banks, that cut it in two parts;
Over the which four stately bridges lean,
That makes safe passage to each part of Rome.

---

13 *learned Maro* The poet Virgil (Publius Virgilius Maro) was buried in Naples in
    19 B.C., and posthumously acquired some reputation as a magician. His tomb
    stands at the end of the promontory of Posilippo between Naples and Pozzuoli;
    legend ascribes the tunnel running through this promontory to his magic art
16 *and the rest* B tries to be more precise with 'to the east', but there is no clear
    sense of direction
17-18 *a sumptuous temple* St Mark's in Venice; details of the mosaics and the
    gilded roof are supplied by *EFB*, and have been incorporated into the B Text:
>   Whose frame is paved with sundry coloured stones,
>   And roofed aloft with curious work in gold.

    But St Mark's has no *aspiring top*, unless the nearby campanile is intended
21 *erst* earlier
23 *Faustus, I have* From this point the A and B Texts are only occasionally similar;
    B's version of the remainder of the scene is printed in the Appendix
31-2 The lines are supplied in the B Text to supply an obvious deficiency in A (the
    'stately bridges' must have something to lean over)

Upon the bridge called Ponte Angelo   35
Erected is a castle passing strong,
Within whose walls such store of ordinance are,
And double cannons, framed of carved brass,
As match the days within one complete year;
Besides the gates, and high pyramides   40
Which Julius Caesar brought from Africa.

FAUSTUS
Now by the kingdoms of infernal rule,
Of Styx, Acheron, and the fiery lake
Of ever-burning Phlegethon, I swear
That I do long to see the monuments   45
And situation of bright-splendent Rome.
Come therefore, let's away.

MEPHASTOPHILIS
Nay Faustus stay, I know you'd fain see the pope,
And take some part of holy Peter's feast,
Where thou shalt see a troup of bald-pate friars,   50
Whose *summum bonum* is in belly-cheer.

FAUSTUS
Well, I am content to compass then some sport,
And by their folly make us merriment.
Then charm me that I may be invisible, to do what I please
unseen of any whilst I stay in Rome.   55

MEPHASTOPHILIS [*casts a spell on him*]
So Faustus, now do what thou wilt, thou shall not be
discerned.

Sound a sennet; enter the POPE *and the* CARDINAL OF LORRAINE
to the banquet, with FRIARS *attending*

35–6 *Upon . . . strong* The Ponte Angelo was built in A.D. 135 by Hadrian, whose
    mausoleum (directly facing the bridge but never standing on it) became the
    Castello di S. Angelo
38 *double cannons* cannons of very high calibre
40–1 *pyramides . . . Africa* the obelisk that stands in front of St Peter's; it was in
    fact brought from Egypt by the emperor Caligula. The plural form *pyramides* is
    often used for the singular: here the extra syllable is needed for the regular
    pentameter
43–4 *Styx . . . Phlegethon* the rivers in Hades, the Greek underworld
46 *situation* lay-out
    bright-splendent resplendent
51 *summum bonum* greatest good; in scholastic theology this is a term used to
    describe the Almighty
52 *compass* take part in

POPE
  My lord of Lorraine, will't please you draw near.
FAUSTUS
  Fall to; and the devil choke you and you spare.
POPE
  How now, who's that which spake? Friars, look about.   60
1 FRIAR
  Here's nobody, if it like your holiness.
POPE
  My lord, here is a dainty dish was sent to me from the
  bishop of Milan.
FAUSTUS
  I thank you, sir.   *Snatch it*
POPE
  How now, who's that which snatched the meat from me?   65
  Will no man look? My lord, this dish was sent me from the
  cardinal of Florence.
FAUSTUS
  You say true? I'll have't.   [*Snatch it*]
POPE
  What, again! My lord, I'll drink to your grace.
FAUSTUS
  I'll pledge your grace.   [*Snatch the cup*]   70
LORRAINE
  My lord, it may be some ghost newly crept out of purgatory
  come to beg a pardon of your holiness.
POPE
  It may be so; friars, prepare a dirge to lay the fury of this
  ghost. Once again my lord, fall to.
                              The POPE *crosseth himself*
FAUSTUS
  What, are you crossing of your self? Well, use that trick no   75
  more, I would advise you.
                                              Cross again

59 *Fall to* get on with it
    and if
70 *pledge* toast
72 *pardon* papal indulgence
73 *dirge* a corruption of *dirige*, which starts the antiphon at Matins in the Office for
    the Dead; hence any requiem mass. The word is used correctly here by the pope,
    but the ritual performed is not in fact a mass but a formal cursing
74 s.d. *crosseth himself* EFB describes how the pope 'would ever be blessing and
    crossing over his mouth'

FAUSTUS
Well, there's the second time; aware the third! I give you
fair warning.

Cross again, and FAUSTUS *hits him a box of the ear,*
and they all run away

FAUSTUS
Come on Mephastophilis, what shall we do?
MEPHASTOPHILIS
Nay, I know not; we shall be cursed with bell, book, and   80
candle.
FAUSTUS
How! Bell, book, and candle; candle, book, and bell,
Forward and backward, to curse Faustus to hell.
Anon you shall hear a hog grunt, a calf bleat, and an ass
bray,
Because it is St Peter's holy day.   85

Enter all the FRIARS *to sing the Dirge*

1 FRIAR
Come brethren, let's about our business with good devo-
tion.
                                                    Sing this
Cursed be he that stole away his holiness' meat from the
table.
          Maledicat Dominus.
Cursed be he that struck his holiness a blow on the face.   90
          Maledicat Dominus.
Cursed be he that took Friar Sandelo a blow on the pate.
          Maledicat Dominus.
Cursed be he that disturbeth our holy dirge.
          Maledicat Dominus.   95
Cursed be he that took away his holiness' wine.
          Maledicat dominus.
              Et omnes sancti. Amen.
                  Beat the Friars, and fling fireworks among
                                    them, and so Exeunt

80-1 *bell, book, and candle* At the close of the Office of Excommunication the bell
    is tolled, the bible closed, and the candle extinguished
89 *Maledicat Dominus* May the Lord curse him
92 *Sandelo* the name probably suggested by the friar's sandals
98 *et omnes sancti* and all the saints

Scene 8

Enter ROBIN *and* RAFE *with a silver goblet*

ROBIN

Come Rafe, did not I tell thee we were for ever made by
this Doctor Faustus' book? *Ecce signum!* Here's a simple
purchase for horse-keepers: our horses shall eat no hay as
long as this lasts.

Enter the VINTNER

RAFE

But Robin, here comes the vintner.   5

ROBIN

Hush, I'll gull him supernaturally! Drawer, I hope all is
paid; God be with you. Come, Rafe.

VINTNER

Soft sir, a word with you. I must yet have a goblet paid
from you ere you go.

ROBIN

I a goblet, Rafe! I a goblet? I scorn you: and you are but a   10
&c . . . I a goblet? Search me.

VINTNER

I mean so, sir, with your favour.   [*Searches* ROBIN]

ROBIN

How say you now?

VINTNER

I must say somewhat to your fellow; you sir!

RAFE

Me sir! Me sir? Search your fill. Now sir, you may be   15
ashamed to burden honest men with a matter of truth.

VINTNER   [*Searches* RAFE]

Well, t'one of you hath this goblet about you.

ROBIN

You lie, drawer; 'tis afore me. Sirra you, I'll teach ye to
impeach honest men; [*to* RAFE] stand by. [*to the* VINTNER]

Scene 8 The B Text version of this scene is printed in the Appendix

   2 *Ecce signum* behold the proof – a fairly common catchword amongst Elizabethan
     comic actors: cf. *1 Henry IV*, where Falstaff shows his 'sword hack'd like a
     handsaw – *ecce signum*' (II, iv, 168)

   2-3 *simple purchase* clear profit

   6 *gull* trick

   10-11 *but a &c* this gives the actor permission for ad-lib terms of abuse

I'll scour you for a goblet – stand aside, you were best – I 20
charge you in the name of Belzebub – look to the goblet,
Rafe!

VINTNER
What mean you, sirra?

ROBIN
I'll tell you what I mean: [*He reads*] *Sanctobulorum
Periphrasticon* – nay, I'll tickle you, vintner – look to the 25
goblet, Rafe – *Polypragmos Belseborams framanto pacosti-
phos tostis Mephastophilis, &c* ...

    Enter MEPHASTOPHILIS: *sets squibs at their backs:
they run about*

VINTNER
O nomine Domine! What mean'st thou Robin? Thou hast
no goblet.

RAFE
Peccatum peccatorum! Here's thy goblet, good Vintner. 30

ROBIN
Misericordia pro nobis! What shall I do? Good devil, forgive
me now, and I'll never rob thy library more.

    Enter to them (again) MEPHASTOPHILIS

MEPHASTOPHILIS
Vanish villains, th'one like an ape, an other like a bear, the
third an ass, for doing this enterprise.

                         Exit VINTNER
Monarch of hell, under whose black survey 35
Great potentates do kneel with awful fear;
Upon whose altars thousand souls do lie;
How am I vexed with these villains' charms!
From Constantinople am I hither come,
Only for pleasure of these damned slaves. 40

ROBIN
How, from Constantinople? You have had a great journey!
Will you take sixpence in your purse to pay for your
supper, and be gone?

24–7 The dog-Latin marks the clowns' attempts to protect themselves from the
devil
32 s.d. *Enter to them* Boas suggests that the script must allow for alternative
endings to the scene – but this seems unnecessary. It would be in proper
medieval tradition for the devil to carry off the Vintner; he could then return to
deal with Robin and Rafe (who, after all, are the real offenders)

MEPHASTOPHILIS

Well villains, for your presumption, I transform thee into
an ape, and thee into a dog; and so begone!   45

Exit

ROBIN

How, into an ape? That's brave: I'll have fine sport with the
boys; I'll get nuts and apples enow.

RAFE

And I must be a dog.

ROBIN

I'faith, thy head will never be out of the potage pot.

Exeunt

[handwritten annotation: The devil makes them pay for using Faustus' powers]

Chorus 3

Enter CHORUS [WAGNER]

CHORUS

When Faustus had with pleasure ta'en the view
Of rarest things, and royal courts of kings,
He stayed his course, and so returned home;
Where such as bare his absence but with grief –
I mean his friends and nearest companions –   5
Did gratulate his safety with kind words.
And in their conference of what befell,
Touching his journey through the world and air,
They put forth questions of astrology,
Which Faustus answered with such learned skill,   10
As they admired and wondered at his wit.
Now is his fame spread forth in every land:
Amongst the rest the emperor is one,
Carolus the fifth, at whose palace now
Faustus is feasted 'mongst his noblemen.   15
What there he did in trial of his art
I leave untold: your eyes shall see performed.

Exit

[handwritten annotation: he is now world renowned]

---

49 *potage* porridge
Chorus 3 The B Text has no trace of this Chorus, which is obviously intended to
    move the play's main action from the papal to the imperial court
  14 *Carolus* Charles V (1519–56), whose court was at Innsbruck

[Scene 9]

Enter EMPEROR, FAUSTUS, *and a* KNIGHT,
with Attendants

EMPEROR
   Master Doctor Faustus, I have heard strange report of thy
   knowledge in the black art, how that none in my empire,
   nor in the whole world, can compare with thee for the rare
   effects of magic. They say thou hast a familiar spirit, by
   whom thou canst accomplish what thou list! This therefore   5
   is my request: that thou let me see some proof of thy skill,
   that mine eyes may be witnesses to confirm what mine ears
   have heard reported. And here I swear to thee, by the
   honour of mine imperial crown, that whatever thou dost,
   thou shalt be in no ways prejudiced or endamaged.   10
KNIGHT (*aside*)
   I'faith, he looks much like a conjuror.
FAUSTUS
   My gracious sovereign, though I must confess myself far
   inferior to the report men have published, and nothing
   answerable to the honour of your imperial majesty, yet for
   that love and duty binds me thereunto, I am content to do   15
   whatsoever your majesty shall command me.
EMPEROR
   Then Doctor Faustus, mark what I shall say. As I was
   sometime solitary set within my closet, sundry thoughts
   arose about the honour of mine ancestors – how they had
   won by prowess such exploits, got such riches, subdued so   20
   many kingdoms, as we that do succeed, or they that shall
   hereafter possess our throne, shall (I fear me) never attain
   to that degree of high renown and great authority. Amongst
   which kings is Alexander the Great, chief spectacle of the
   world's pre-eminence: 25
   The bright shining of whose glorious acts
   Lightens the world with his reflecting beams;
   As when I hear but motion made of him,
   It grieves my soul I never saw the man.
   If therefore thou, by cunning of thine art,   30

Scene 9 B's much-expanded version of this scene is printed in the Appendix
   18 *set* sitting
   24 *Alexander the Great* Alexander III of Macedon (356–323 B.C.)
   28 *motion* mention

(handwritten marginal note: asks Faustus to raise up Alexander the Great & his wife *)*

Canst raise this man from hollow vaults below,
Where lies entombed this famous conqueror,
And bring with him his beauteous paramour,
Both in their right shapes, gesture, and attire
They used to wear during their time of life,   35
Thou shalt both satisfy my just desire,
And give me cause to praise thee whilst I live.

FAUSTUS
My gracious lord, I am ready to accomplish your request,
so far forth as by art and power of my spirit I am able to
perform.   40

KNIGHT (*aside*)
I'faith, that's just nothing at all.

FAUSTUS
But, if it like your grace, it is not in my ability to present
before your eyes the true substantial bodies of those two
deceased princes which long since are consumed to dust.

KNIGHT (*aside*)
Ay, marry, master doctor, now there's a sign of grace in   45
you, when you will confess the truth.

FAUSTUS
But such spirits as can lively resemble Alexander and his
paramour shall appear before your grace, in that manner
that they best lived in, in their most flourishing estate:
which I doubt not shall sufficiently content your imperial   50
majesty.

EMPEROR
Go to, master doctor, let me see them presently.

KNIGHT
Do you hear, master doctor? You bring Alexander and his
paramour before the emperor!

FAUSTUS
How then, sir?   55

KNIGHT
I'faith, that's as true as Diana turned me to a stag.

FAUSTUS
No sir; but when Actaeon died, he left the horns for you!
Mephastophilis, begone!

Exit MEPHASTOPHILIS

---

33 *paramour* probably Roxana, Alexander's wife
57 *Actaeon* As a punishment for coming upon the goddess Diana and her nymphs
when they were bathing, Actaeon was turned into a stag, and his own hounds
tore him to pieces

KNIGHT

Nay, and you go to conjuring I'll be gone.

Exit KNIGHT

FAUSTUS

I'll meet with you anon for interrupting me so. Here they   60
are, my gracious lord.

Enter MEPHASTOPHILIS
with ALEXANDER *and his* PARAMOUR

EMPEROR

Master doctor, I heard this lady, while she lived, had a wart
or mole in her neck; how shall I know whether it be so or
no?

FAUSTUS

Your highness may boldly go and see.   65

[*The* EMPEROR *examines the lady's neck*]

EMPEROR

Sure, these are no spirits, but the true substantial bodies of
those two deceased princes.

Exit ALEXANDER [*and his* PARAMOUR]

FAUSTUS

Will't please your highness now to send for the knight that
was so pleasant with me here of late?

EMPEROR

One of you call him forth.   70

Enter the KNIGHT *with a pair of horns on his head*

EMPEROR

How now sir knight? Why, I had thought thou hadst been a
bachelor, but now I see thou hast a wife that not only gives
thee horns but makes thee wear them! Feel on thy head.

KNIGHT

Thou damned wretch and execrable dog,
Bred in the concave of some monstrous rock,   75
How dar'st thou thus abuse a gentleman?
Villain I say, undo what thou hast done.

FAUSTUS

O not so fast sir, there's no haste but good. Are you

72-3 *wife . . . wear them* It was an old joke that the cuckolded husband would grow
  horns to publish his shame
75 *Bred . . . rock* cf. 2 *Tamburlaine*, III, ii, 89: 'Fenc'd with the concave of some
  monstrous rock'
78-9 *Are you remembered* Have you forgotten

remembered how you crossed me in my conference with
the emperor? I think I have met with you for it.   80
EMPEROR
Good master doctor, at my entreaty release him; he hath
done penance sufficient.
FAUSTUS
My gracious lord, not so much for the injury he offered me
here in your presence, as to delight you with some mirth,
hath Faustus worthily requited this injurious knight; which   85
being all I desire, I am content to release him of his horns.
And, sir knight, hereafter speak well of scholars: Mephastophilis, transform him straight. Now my good lord, having
done my duty, I humbly take my leave.
EMPEROR
Farewell master doctor; yet ere you go, expect from me a   90
bounteous reward.

                          Exit EMPEROR [*and his Attendants*]
FAUSTUS
Now Mephastophilis, the restless course
That time doth run with calm and silent foot,
Shortening my days and thread of vital life,
Calls for the payment of my latest years;   95
Therefore, sweet Mephastophilis, let us make haste to
                                                Wittenberg.
MEPHASTOPHILIS
What, will you go on horseback, or on foot?
FAUSTUS
Nay, till I am past this fair and pleasant green, I'll walk on
foot.

shows his powers

94 *thread of vital life* The image of life as a single thread comes from Greek
   mythology
95 *payment* The idea of death as a debt owed to nature is a commonplace (cf.
   Macbeth, V,ix, 5: 'Your son, my lord, has paid a soldier's debt'); but it is
   revitalized here by Faustus' predicament
   latest last

[Scene 10]

Enter [to them] a HORSE-COURSER

HORSE-COURSER
  I have been all this day seeking one Master Fustian: 'mass,
  see where he is! God save you, master doctor.
FAUSTUS
  What, horse-courser: you are well met.
HORSE-COURSER
  Do you hear, sir; I have brought you forty dollars for your
  horse.   5
FAUSTUS
  I cannot sell him so: if thou lik'st him for fifty, take him.
HOURSE-COURSER
  Alas sir, I have no more. I pray you speak for me.
MEPHASTOPHILIS
  I pray you let him have him; he is an honest fellow, and he
  has a great charge – neither wife nor child.
FAUSTUS
  Well; come, give me your money; my boy will deliver him   10
  to you. But I must tell you one thing before you have him:
  ride him not into the water at any hand.
HORSE-COURSER
  Why sir, will he not drink of all waters?
FAUSTUS
  O yes, he will drink of all waters, but ride him not into the
  water. Ride him over hedge or ditch, or where thou wilt,   15
  but not into the water.
HORSE-COURSER
  Well sir. Now am I made man for ever: I'll not leave my

Scene 10 The B Text version of this scene is printed in the Appendix
s.d. *Horse-courser* Horse-dealer; a reputation for dishonesty has always attached to
    such traders
  1 *Fustian* the Horse-courser's mispronunciation of 'Faustus' – and perhaps a
    suggestion that the role was once doubled with that of the Clown who in Scene 4
    commented that Wagner spoke 'Dutch fustian'
 12 *not into the water* Running water dissolves a witch's spell
    at any hand whatever happens
 13 *drink of all waters* go anywhere
 17 *leave* part with

horse for forty! If he had but the quality of hey ding ding,
hey ding ding, I'd make a brave living on him! He has a
buttock as slick as an eel. Well, God b'y sir; your boy will   20
deliver him me. But hark ye sir, if my horse be sick, or ill at
ease, if I bring his water to you, you'll tell me what it is?

Exit HORSE-COURSER

FAUSTUS

Away, you villain! What, dost think I am a horse-doctor?
What art thou, Faustus, but a man condemned to die?
Thy fatal time doth draw to final end.   25
Despair doth drive distrust unto my thoughts:
Confound these passions with a quiet sleep.
Tush, Christ did call the thief upon the cross;
Then rest thee, Faustus, quiet in conceit.

Sleep in his chair

Enter HORSE-COURSER *all wet, crying*

HORSE-COURSER

Alas, alas, Doctor Fustian, quoth 'a: 'mass, Doctor Lopus   30
was never such a doctor! H'as given me a purgation, h'as
purged me of forty dollars! I shall never see them more. But
yet, like an ass as I was, I would not be ruled by him; for he
bade me I should ride him into no water. Now I, thinking
my horse had had some rare quality that he would not have   35
had me known of, I, like a vent'rous youth, rid him into the
deep pond at the town's end. I was no sooner in the middle
of the pond, but my horse vanished away, and I sat upon a
bottle of hay, never so near drowning in my life! But I'll
seek out my doctor, and have my forty dollars again, or I'll   40
make it the dearest horse. O, yonder is his snipper-snapper!
Do you hear, you hey-pass, where's your master?

18 *for forty* for any amount of money
   quality of hey ding ding The Horse-courser seems to be wishing that the horse
   were a stallion, not a gelding; cf. Nashe, *Have With You to Saffron Walden*
   (1596): 'Yea, Madam *Gabriele*, are you such an old ierker? then Hey ding a
   ding, vp with your petticoate, haue at your plum-tree' (McKerrow iii, p. 113)
22 *his water* his urine (for diagnosis)
28 *Christ...cross* St Luke's Gospel tells of Christ's words of comfort to the
   crucified thief: 'This day shalt thou be with me in paradise' (xxiii, 43)
29 *in conceit* in this thought
30 *Doctor Lopus* This joke must have found its way into the text after the
   execution, in February 1594, of Roderigo Lopez, Queen Elizabeth's personal
   physician, who was accused of plotting to poison Her Majesty
39 *bottle* truss
42 *hey-pass* a conjuror's 'magic' catchphrase

The man didn't listen to Faustus & the horse vanished in water

MEPHASTOPHILIS

Why sir, what would you? You cannot speak with him.

HORSE-COURSER

But I will speak with him.

MEPHASTOPHILIS

Why, he's fast asleep; come some other time.   45

HORSE-COURSER

I'll speak with him now, or I'll break his glass-windows about his ears.

MEPHASTOPHILIS

I tell thee, he has not slept this eight nights.

HORSE-COURSER

And he has not slept this eight weeks I'll speak with him.   50

MEPHASTOPHILIS

See where he is, fast asleep.

HORSE-COURSER

Ay, this is he; God save ye master doctor, master doctor, master Doctor Fustian, forty dollars, forty dollars for a bottle of hay.

MEPHASTOPHILIS

Why, thou seest he hears thee not.   55

HORSE-COURSER

So ho ho; so ho ho.

                          Halloo in his ear

No, will you not wake? I'll make you wake ere I go.

               Pull him by the leg, and pull it away

Alas, I am undone! What shall I do?

FAUSTUS

O my leg, my leg! Help, Mephastophilis! Call the officers! My leg, my leg!   60

MEPHASTOPHILIS

Come villain, to the constable.

HORSE-COURSER

O Lord, sir! Let me go, and I'll give you forty dollars more.

MEPHASTOPHILIS

Where be they?

HORSE-COURSER

I have none about me: come to my ostry and I'll give them you.   65

---

46 *glass-windows* spectacles
56 *So ho ho* the huntsman's cry when he catches sight of the quarry
64 *ostry* hostelry, inn

MEPHASTOPHILIS

Begone quickly!

HORSE-COURSER runs away

FAUSTUS

What, is he gone? Farewell he: Faustus has his leg again,
and the horse-courser – I take it – a bottle of hay for his
labour! Well, this trick shall cost him forty dollars more.

Enter WAGNER

How now Wagner, what's the news with thee?   70

WAGNER

Sir, the Duke of Vanholt doth earnestly entreat your
company.

FAUSTUS

The Duke of Vanholt! An honourable gentleman, to whom
I must be no niggard of my cunning. Come Mephastophilis,
let's away to him.   75

Exeunt

[Scene 11]

[FAUSTUS *and* MEPHASTOPHILIS *return to the stage.*
Enter to them the DUKE *and the* DUCHESS;
the DUKE *speaks*

DUKE

Believe me, master doctor, this merriment hath much
pleased me.

FAUSTUS

My gracious Lord, I am glad it contents you so well: but it
may be, madam, you take no delight in this; I have heard
that great-bellied women do long for some dainties or   5
other – what is it, madam? Tell me, and you shall have it.

DUCHESS

Thanks, good master doctor; and for I see your courteous
intent to pleasure me, I will not hide from you the thing my

Scene 11 In the B Text this scene is expanded, but not substantially altered. It is
    preceded by a tavern scene, where the clowns narrate some of the Doctor's
    trickeries, and followed by an episode which merges the court and the tavern so
    that Faustus can play another trick on the clowns
s.d. *Enter to them* On the printed page this seems to be a clumsy way of linking two
    episodes, but on the stage there is no problem

heart desires. And were it now summer, as it is January and
the dead of winter, I would desire no better meat than a   10
dish of ripe grapes.

FAUSTUS

Alas madam, that's nothing! Mephastophilis, begone!

Exit MEPHASTOPHILIS

Were it a greater thing than this, so it would content you,
you should have it.

Enter MEPHASTOPHILIS *with the grapes*

Here they be, madam; will't please you taste on them?   15

DUKE

Believe me, master doctor, this makes me wonder above the
rest: that being in the dead time of winter, and in the month
of January, how you should come by these grapes?

FAUSTUS

If it like your grace, the year is divided into two circles over
the whole world, that when it is here winter with us, in the   20
contrary circle it is summer with them, as in India, Saba,
and farther countries in the east; and by means of a swift
spirit that I have, I had them brought hither, as ye see. How
do you like them, madam; be they good?

DUCHESS

Believe me, master doctor, they be the best grapes that ere I   25
tasted in my life before.

FAUSTUS

I am glad they content you so, madam.

DUKE

Come madam, let us in, where you must well reward this
learned man for the great kindness he hath showed to you.

DUCHESS

And so I will my lord; and whilst I live, rest beholding for   30
this courtesy.

FAUSTUS

I humbly thank your grace.

DUKE

Come, master doctor, follow us, and receive your reward.

Exeunt

---

19 *two circles* The explanation is confusing. The relevant circles would be the
   northern and southern hemispheres, but the author appears to be thinking in
   terms of east and west; *EFB* evades the matter while providing the detail of the
   twice-yearly fruit

21 *Saba* Sheba; in modern times, this is the Yemen

he is again called een luy gaut afficials to see his power

[Chorus 4]

Enter WAGNER *solus*

WAGNER
    I think my master means to die shortly,
    For he hath given to me all his goods!
    And yet methinks, if that death were near,
    He would not banquet, and carouse, and swill,
    Amongst the students, as even now he doth,   5
    Who are at supper with such belly-cheer,
    As Wagner ne'er beheld in all his life.
    See where they come: belike the feast is ended.

                                                       [*Exit*]

[Scene 12]

Enter FAUSTUS [*and* MEPHASTOPHILIS],
with two or three SCHOLARS

1 SCHOLAR
    Master Doctor Faustus, since our conference about fair
    ladies, which was the beautifullest in all the world, we have
    determined with ourselves that Helen of Greece was the
    admirablest lady that ever lived. Therefore, master doctor,
    if you will do us that favour as to let us see that peerless   5
    dame of Greece, whom all the world admires for majesty,
    we should think ourselves much beholding unto you.
FAUSTUS
    Gentlemen, for that I know your friendship is unfeigned,
    And Faustus' custom is not to deny
    The just requests of those that wish him well,   10
    You shall behold that peerless dame of Greece,

Chorus Again, the direction for Wagner's entrance suggests that the choric figure
    doubled with the role of Faustus' servant
   1–8 In place of these lines, B gives Wagner a prose speech containing the gist of
    A's verse
Scene 12 The A and B versions of this scene are closely related; but B is markedly
    inferior to A, reading like a poor memorial reconstruction of the Scholars' lines,
    but having a re-written speech for the Old Man
   3 *Helen of Greece* Helen (who was married to Menelaus, king of Sparta) was given
    to Paris as a reward for judging the contest of three goddesses
   8–15 as prose in A

No otherways for pomp and majesty
Than when Sir Paris crossed the seas with her,
And brought the spoils to rich Dardania.
Be silent then, for danger is in words.   15

Music sounds, and HELEN *passeth over the stage*

2 SCHOLAR
Too simple is my wit to tell her praise,
Whom all the world admires for majesty.
3 SCHOLAR
No marvel though the angry Greeks pursued
With ten years' war the rape of such a queen,
Whose heavenly beauty passeth all compare.   20
1 SCHOLAR
Since we have seen the pride of Nature's works,
And only paragon of excellence,
Let us depart; and for this glorious deed
Happy and blest be Faustus evermore.
FAUSTUS
Gentlemen farewell; the same I wish to you.   25

Exeunt SCHOLARS

Enter an OLD MAN

OLD MAN
Ah Doctor Faustus, that I might prevail
To guide thy steps unto the way of life,

14 *Dardania* Troy; in fact the city built by Dardanus on the Hellespont, but the
   name is often transferred to Troy
15 s.d. *passeth over* It would appear that the character was instructed to move from
   one side of the yard, across the stage, and out at the other side of the yard,
   instead of entering by the stage doors (cf. Allardyce Nicoll, 'Passing Over the
   Stage', *Shakespeare Survey*, XII [1959], pp. 47–55)
16–24 In the B Text the Scholars' comments are as follows:
   2 SCHOLAR
      Was this fair Helen, whose admired worth
      Made Greece with ten years' war afflict poor Troy?
   3 SCHOLAR
      Too simple is my wit to tell her worth,
      Whom all the world admires for majesty.
   1 SCHOLAR
      Now we have seen the pride of Nature's work,
      We'll take our leaves, and for this blessed sight
      Happy and blest be Faustus evermore.
26–37 The Old Man's speech is oddly strained: a 'goal' cannot 'conduct', and
   'commiseration' does not 'expel'; the speech seems to have been re-written for
   the B Text – see the Appendix

By which sweet path thou may'st attain the goal
That shall conduct thee to celestial rest.
Break heart, drop blood, and mingle it with tears,
Tears falling from repentant heaviness
Of thy most vile and loathsome filthiness,
The stench whereof corrupts the inward soul
With such flagitious crimes of heinous sins,
As no commiseration may expel;   35
But mercy, Faustus, of thy saviour sweet,
Whose blood alone must wash away thy guilt.

FAUSTUS
Where art thou Faustus? Wretch, what hast thou done!
Damned art thou Faustus, damned; despair and die!

MEPHASTOPHILIS *gives him a dagger*

Hell calls for right, and with a roaring voice   40
Says, 'Faustus, come: thine hour is come'!
And Faustus will come to do thee right.

OLD MAN
Ah stay, good Faustus, stay thy desperate steps!
I see an angel hovers o'er thy head,
And with a vial full of precious grace   45
Offers to pour the same into thy soul!
Then call for mercy, and avoid despair.

FAUSTUS
Ah my sweet friend, I feel thy words
To comfort my distressed soul;
Leave me awhile to ponder on my sins.   50

OLD MAN
I go, sweet Faustus; but with heavy cheer,
Fearing the ruin of thy hopeless soul.   [*Exit*]

FAUSTUS
Accursed Faustus, where is mercy now?
I do repent, and yet I do despair:
Hell strives with grace for conquest in my breast!   55
What shall I do to shun the snares of death?

MEPHASTOPHILIS
Thou traitor, Faustus: I arrest thy soul
For disobedience to my sovereign lord.
Revolt, or I'll in piecemeal tear thy flesh.

FAUSTUS
Sweet Mephastophilis, entreat thy lord
To pardon my unjust presumption;   60

59 *Revolt* Turn again to your allegiance

And with my blood again I will confirm
My former vow I made to Lucifer.
MEPHASTOPHILIS
Do it then quickly, with unfeigned heart,
Lest greater danger do attend thy drift.	65
FAUSTUS
Torment, sweet friend, that base and crooked age
That durst dissuade me from thy Lucifer,
With greatest torments that our hell affords.
MEPHASTOPHILIS
His faith is great, I cannot touch his soul,
But what I may afflict his body with,	70
I will attempt – which is but little worth.
FAUSTUS
One thing, good servant, let me crave of thee,
To glut the longing of my heart's desire:
That I might have unto my paramour
That heavenly Helen which I saw of late,	75
Whose sweet embracings may extinguish clean
These thoughts that do dissuade me from my vow:
And keep mine oath I made to Lucifer.
MEPHASTOPHILIS
Faustus, this, or what else thou shalt desire,
Shall be performed in twinkling of an eye.	80

Enter HELEN

FAUSTUS
Was this the face that launched a thousand ships,
And burnt the topless towers of Ilium?
Sweet Helen, make me immortal with a kiss:
Her lips sucks forth my soul, see where it flies!
Come Helen, come, give me my soul again.	85

65 *drift* drifting; also purpose
81–100 In these lines Marlowe is repeating his own memorable phrases:
Helen, whose beauty summoned Greece to arms,
And drew a thousand ships to Tenedos.
2 Tamburlaine, II,iv, 87–8
And he'll make me immortal with a kiss.
Dido, IV,iv, 123
So thou wouldst prove as true as Paris did,
Would, as fair Troy was, Carthage might be sacked,
And I be called a second Helena.
Dido, V,i, 146–8
82 *Ilium* Troy

Here will I dwell, for heaven be in these lips,
And all is dross that is not Helena!

Enter OLD MAN

I will be Paris, and for love of thee,
Instead of Troy shall Wittenberg be sacked;
And I will combat with weak Menelaus,   90
And wear thy colours on my plumed crest:
Yea, I will wound Achilles in the heel,
And then return to Helen for a kiss.
O thou art fairer than the evening air,
Clad in the beauty of a thousand stars,   95
Brighter art thou than flaming Jupiter
When he appeared to hapless Semele;
More lovely than the monarch of the sky
In wanton Arethusa's azured arms;
And none but thou shalt be my paramour.   100

Exeunt [FAUSTUS *and* HELEN]

OLD MAN
Accursed Faustus, miserable man,
That from thy soul exclud'st the grace of heaven,
And fliest the throne of His tribunal seat!

Enter the DEVILS

Satan begins to sift me with his pride,
As in this furnace God shall try my faith.   105
My faith, vile hell, shall triumph over thee!
Ambitious fiends, see how the heavens smiles
At your repulse, and laughs your state to scorn.
Hence hell, for hence I fly unto my God.

Exeunt

88 s.d. This direction and the Old Man's final speech (101–9) are omitted in the B
Text
92 *wound . . . heel* Achilles was invulnerable apart from one of his heels – where he
was shot by Paris
96–7 *flaming . . . Semele* The sight of Jupiter in all his divine splendour was too
much for mortal eyes, and Semele was consumed by the fire of his brightness
98–9 *monarch . . . arms* Arethusa was a nymph who was changed into a fountain
after bathing in the river Alpheus and exciting the river-god's passion; Alpheus
is said to have been related to the sun
104 *sift* Cf. St Luke's Gospel xxii, 3: 'Satan hath desired to have you, that he may sift
you as wheat'
107 *the heavens* the celestial beings who inhabit the extra-terrestrial spheres of the
geocentric universe
smiles A singular verb following a plural subject is not uncommon in sixteenth-
century literature

[Scene 13]

Enter FAUSTUS *with the* SCHOLARS

FAUSTUS
Ah gentlemen!
1 SCHOLAR
What ails Faustus?
FAUSTUS
Ah my sweet chamber-fellow, had I lived with thee, then
had I lived still; but now I die eternally. Look, comes he
not, comes he not?   5
2 SCHOLAR
What means Faustus?
3 SCHOLAR
Belike he is grown into some sickness, by being over-
solitary.
1 SCHOLAR
If it be so, we'll have physicians to cure him; 'tis but a
surfeit: never fear, man.   10
FAUSTUS
A surfeit of deadly sin, that hath damned both body and
soul.
2 SCHOLAR
Yet Faustus, look up to heaven; remember God's mercies
are infinite.
FAUSTUS
But Faustus' offence can ne'er be pardoned! The serpent   15
that tempted Eve may be saved, but not Faustus. Ah
gentlemen, hear me with patience, and tremble not at my
speeches, though my heart pants and quivers to remember
that I have been a student here these thirty years – O would
I had never seen Wittenberg, never read book – and what   20
wonders I have done, all Wittenberg can witness – yea, all
the world; for which Faustus hath lost both Germany and
the world – yea, heaven itself – heaven, the seat of God, the
throne of the blessed, the kingdom of joy; and must remain
in hell for ever – hell, ah, hell for ever! Sweet friends, what 25
shall become of Faustus, being in hell for ever?
3 SCHOLAR
Yet Faustus, call on God.

Scene 13 B opens this scene with the arrival of the devils – Lucifer, Belzebub, and
   Mephastophilis – who have come to witness Faustus' end; see the Appendix

FAUSTUS

On God, whom Faustus hath abjured? On God, whom
Faustus hath blasphemed? Ah my God – I would weep, but
the devil draws in my tears! gush forth blood instead of 30
tears – yea, life and soul! O, he stays my tongue! I would lift
up my hands, but see, they hold them, they hold them!

ALL

Who, Faustus?

FAUSTUS

Lucifer and Mephastophilis! Ah gentlemen, I gave them my
soul for my cunning. 35

ALL

God forbid!

FAUSTUS

God forbade it indeed, but Faustus hath done it: for the
vain pleasure of four-and-twenty years hath Faustus lost
eternal joy and felicity! I writ them a bill with mine own
blood, the date is expired, the time will come, and he will 40
fetch me.

1 SCHOLAR

Why did not Faustus tell us of this before, that divines
might have prayed for thee?

FAUSTUS

Oft have I thought to have done so, but the devil threatened
to tear me in pieces if I named God, to fetch both body and 45
soul, if I once gave ear to divinity; and now 'tis too late!
Gentlemen away, lest you perish with me.

2 SCHOLAR

O what shall we do to save Faustus?

3 SCHOLAR

God will strengthen me. I will stay with Faustus.

1 SCHOLAR

Tempt not God, sweet friend, but let us into the next room, 50
and there pray for him.

FAUSTUS

Ay, pray for me, pray for me; and what noise soever ye
hear, come not unto me, for nothing can rescue me.

30 *draws in my tears* 'No not so much as their eyes are able to shed tears (thretten
and torture them as ye please) while first they repent (God not permitting them
to dissemble their obstinacie in so horrible a crime)', *Daemonologie*, by James
VI and I (Edinburgh, 1597), p. 81
31 *stays* holds back
37–8 *for the vain* B (for vain A)
48 *to save Faustus* B (to Faustus A)

2 SCHOLAR
    Pray thou, and we will pray, that God may have mercy
    upon thee.   55
FAUSTUS
    Gentlemen, farewell. If I live till morning, I'll visit you; if
    not, Faustus is gone to hell.
ALL
    Faustus, farewell.

                                              Exeunt SCHOLARS

                    The clock strikes eleven

FAUSTUS
    Ah Faustus,
    Now hast thou but one bare hour to live,   60
    And then thou must be damned perpetually.
    Stand still, you ever-moving spheres of heaven,
    That time may cease, and midnight never come.
    Fair Nature's eye, rise, rise again, and make
    Perpetual day, or let this hour be but   65
    A year, a month, a week, a natural day,
    That Faustus may repent and save his soul.
    O lente, lente currite noctis equi!
    The stars move still, time runs, the clock will strike,
    The devil will come, and Faustus must be damned.   70
    O I'll leap up to my God! Who pulls me down?
    See, see where Christ's blood streams in the firmament!
    One drop would save my soul, half a drop: ah my Christ –
    Ah, rend not my heart for naming of my Christ;
    Yet will I call on him – O spare me, Lucifer!   75
    Where is it now? 'Tis gone: and see where God

[Handwritten margin note: God is something other than Limited & alienated from God]

58 *Farewell* See the Appendix for the B Text's insertion at this point
62-7 Cf. *Edward II*, V, i, 64–8:
        Continue ever, thou celestial sun;
        Let never silent night possess this clime:
        Stand still, you watches of the element;
        All times and seasons, rest you at a stay,
        That Edward may be still fair England's king.
68 'Go slowly, slowly, you horses of the night': the play's final irony; the line is
    from Ovid's *Amores*, I, xiii, 40, where the poet longs for never-ending night in
    his mistress' arms
71 *leap up ... down* the titlepage of the 1604 edition depicts Faustus' position
    emblematically
76 *it* the vision of Christ's blood; the momentary yielding to terror and the devil
    banishes even this hope of salvation

Stretcheth out his arm, and bends his ireful brows!
Mountains and hills, come, come and fall on me,
And hide me from the heavy wrath of God.
No, no?   80
Then will I headlong run into the earth:
Earth, gape! O no, it will not harbour me.
You stars that reigned at my nativity,
Whose influence hath allotted death and hell,
Now draw up Faustus like a foggy mist   85
Into the entrails of yon labouring cloud,
That when you vomit forth into the air
My limbs may issue from your smoky mouths,
So that my soul may but ascend to heaven.

                    The watch strikes

Ah, half the hour is past: 'twill all be past anon.
O God, if thou wilt not have mercy on my soul,   90
Yet for Christ's sake, whose blood hath ransomed me,
Impose some end to my incessant pain:
Let Faustus live in hell a thousand years,
A hundred thousand, and at last be saved.   95
O, no end is limited to damned souls!
Why wert thou not a creature wanting soul?
Or why is this immortal that thou hast?
Ah, Pythagoras' *metempsychosis* – were that true,
This soul should fly from me, and I be changed   100
Unto some brutish beast:
All beasts are happy, for when they die,
Their souls are soon dissolved in elements;
But mine must live still to be plagued in hell.
Cursed be the parents that engendered me: 105

78-9 'And they shall say to the mountains: Cover us; and to the hills, Fall on us',
   Hosea x, 8 (see also Revelations vi, 16; and St Luke xxiii, 3). The Usurer in *A
   Looking Glass for London* has the same idea:
       Hell gapes for me, heaven will not hold my soule,
       You mountaines shroude me from the God of truth . . .
       Cover me hills, and shroude me from the Lord.
                                              ll. 2054-5, 9
83-9 *You . . . heaven* Faustus prays the stars, whose positions at his birth ordained
   this fate, to suck him up into a cloud, as a fog or mist is drawn up, and then in a
   storm expel his body in order that his soul may be saved. Cf. *1 Tamburlaine*,
   IV, ii, 33: 'Smile, stars that reigned at my nativity'
99 *Pythagoras metempsychosis* the theory of the transmigration of souls, attributed
   to Pythagoras, whereby the human soul at the death of the body took on some
   other form of life

No Faustus, curse thy self, curse Lucifer,
That hath deprived thee of the joys of heaven!
                              The clock striketh twelve
O it strikes, it strikes! Now body, turn to air,
Or Lucifer will bear thee quick to hell.
                              Thunder and lightning
O soul, be changed into little water drops,   110
And fall into the ocean, ne'er be found.
My God, my God, look not so fierce on me!

                    Enter DEVILS

Adders and serpents, let me breathe awhile!
Ugly hell gape not! Come not, Lucifer!
I'll burn my books – ah, Mephastophilis!   115
                              Exeunt with him

              [Epilogue]

          Enter CHORUS

Cut is the branch that might have grown full straight,
And burned is Apollo's laurel bough,
That sometime grew within this learned man.
Faustus is gone! Regard his hellish fall,
Whose fiendful fortune may exhort the wise   5
Only to wonder at unlawful things:
Whose deepness doth entice such forward wits,
To practise more than heavenly power permits.
                              [Exit]

      Terminat hora diem, terminat author opus.

109   *quick* living
115   *burn my books* All magicians who renounced their art made a solemn act of
      disposing of their magic books; cf. *The Tempest*, V, i, 56–7: 'deeper than did ever
      plummet sound I'll drown my book'
115   s.d. *Exeunt with him* The B Text adds a macabre scene where the Scholars
      discover Faustus' mangled body (see the Appendix). Both texts conclude with
      an Epilogue, in the tradition of the Morality Plays
  2   *Apollo's laurel bough* the wreath of the poet (in this case, conjuror – see scene 3,
      line 33) laureate
      Terminat . . . opus The hour ends the day, the author ends his work. The origin
      is unknown, and it seems likely that the motto, with the final emblem, was
      appended by the printer and not by Marlowe
      The Latin motto is followed by another printer's device – McKerrow 313:
      'Framed device of Justice striking a bushel of corn; with SUCH AS I MAKE.
      SUCH WILL I TAKE'

APPENDIX

SCENES FROM THE B Text: sometimes these are straightfor-
ward additions to the play presented in the A Text; in other
cases, the A scenes have been substantially re-worked. The
scenes in the Appendix are identified by the numbers of the
A Text scenes which they replace or augment.

Scene 4

Enter WAGNER *and the* CLOWN

WAGNER
Come hither, sirra boy.

CLOWN
Boy? O disgrace to my person: Zounds, boy in your face,
you have seen many boys with beards, I am sure.

WAGNER
Sirra, hast thou no comings in?

CLOWN
Yes, and goings out too, you may see sir.

WAGNER
Alas poor slave, see how poverty jests in his nakedness. I
know the villain's out of service, and so hungry, that I know
he would give his soul to the devil, for a shoulder of
mutton, tho' it were blood raw.

CLOWN
Not so neither! I had need to have it well roasted, and good
sauce to it, if I pay so dear, I can tell you.

WAGNER
Sirra, wilt thou be my man and wait on me? And I will
make thee go like *Qui mihi discipulus.*

CLOWN
What, in verse?

WAGNER
No slave, in beaten silk and stavesacre.

CLOWN
Stavesacre? That's good to kill vermin: then belike if I
serve you, I shall be lousy.

WAGNER
Why, so thou shalt be, whether thou dost it or no: for sirra,
if thou dost not presently bind thy self to me for seven

years, I'll turn all the lice about thee into familiars, and
make them tear thee in pieces.

CLOWN

Nay sir, you may save yourself a labour, for they are as
familiar with me, as if they paid for their meat and drink, I
can tell you.

WAGNER

Well sirra, leave your jesting, and take these guilders.

CLOWN

Yes, marry sir; and I thank you too.

WAGNER

So; now thou art to be at an hour's warning, whensoever,
and wheresoever the devil shall fetch thee.

CLOWN

Here, take your guilders; I'll none of 'em.

WAGNER

Not I; thou art pressed! Prepare thyself, for I will presently
raise up two devils to carry thee away: Banio, Belcher!

CLOWN

Belcher? and Belcher come here, I'll belch him: I am not
afraid of a devil.

Enter TWO DEVILS

WAGNER

How now, sir; will you serve me now?

CLOWN

Ay, good Wagner; take away the devil, then.

WAGNER

Spirits, away! Now sirra, follow me.

CLOWN

I will, sir! But hark you, master – will you teach me this
conjuring occupation?

WAGNER

Ay sirra, I'll teach thee to turn thyself to a dog, or a cat, or a
mouse, or a rat, or anything.

CLOWN

A dog, or a cat, or a mouse, or a rat? O brave, Wagner!

WAGNER

Villain, call me Master Wagner; and see that you walk
attentively, and let your right eye be always diametrally
fixed upon my left heel, that thou may'st, 'Quasi vestigias
nostras insistere'.

CLOWN

Well sir, I warrant you.

Exeunt

Scene 6

Enter the CLOWN [ROBIN]

ROBIN

What, Dick, look to the horses there till I come again. I
have gotten one of Doctor Faustus' conjuring books, and
now we'll have such knavery as 't passes.

Enter DICK

DICK

What, Robin, you must come away and walk the horses.

ROBIN

I walk the horses! I scorn 't, i'faith. I have other matters in
hand. Let the horses walk themselves and they will. [*Reads*]
'A *per se* a, t. h. e. the; o *per se* o; deny orgon, gorgon'. Keep
further from me, O thou illiterate and unlearned ostler.

DICK

'Snails, what hast thou got there? A book! Why, thou canst
not tell ne'er a word on't.

ROBIN

That thou shalt see presently. Keep out of the circle, I say,
lest I send you into the ostry with a vengeance.

DICK

That's like, 'faith. You had best leave your foolery, for an
my master come, he'll conjure you i'faith.

ROBIN

My master conjure me? I'll tell thee what, an my master
come here, I'll clap as fair a pair of horns on's head as ere
thou saw'st in thy life.

DICK

Thou needst not do that, for my mistress hath done it.

ROBIN

Ay, there be of us here that have waded as deep into
matters as other men, if they were disposed to talk.

DICK

A plague take you. I thought you did not sneak up and
down after her for nothing. But I prithee tell me, in good
sadness Robin, is that a conjuring book?

ROBIN

Do but speak what thou'st have me to do, and I'll do't! If
thou'st dance naked, put off thy clothes and I'll conjure
thee about presently. Or if thou'st go but to the tavern with
me, I'll give thee white wine, red wine, claret wine, sack,

muscadine, malmesy, and whippincrust – hold belly hold –
and we'll not pay one penny for it.

DICK

O brave! Prithee let's to it presently, for I am as dry as a
dog.

ROBIN

Come then, let's away.

Exeunt

Scene 7

MEPHOSTOPHILIS

Nay stay my Faustus, I know you'd see the pope
And take some part of holy Peter's feast,
The which this day with high solemnity,
This day is held through Rome and Italy,
In honour of the pope's triumphant victory.

FAUSTUS

Sweet Mephostophilis, thou pleasest me.
Whilst I am here on earth, let me be cloyed
With all things that delight the heart of man.
My four and twenty years of liberty
I'll spend in pleasure and in dalliance,
That Faustus' name, whilst this bright frame doth stand,
May be admired through the furthest land.

MEPHOSTOPHILIS

'Tis well said Faustus; come then, stand by me,
And thou shalt see them come immediately.

FAUSTUS

Nay, stay, my gentle Mephostophilis,
And grant me my request, and then I go.
Thou know'st within the compass of eight days
We view'd the face of heaven, of earth and hell.
So high our dragons soar'd into the air,
That looking down the earth appeared to me,
No bigger than my hand in quantity.
There did we view the kingdoms of the world,
And what might please mine eye, I there beheld.
Then in this show let me an actor be,
That this proud pope may Faustus' coming see.

MEPHOSTOPHILIS

Let it be so, my Faustus, but first stay,
And view their triumphs, as they pass this way.
And then devise what best contents thy mind,

By cunning in thine art to cross the pope,
Or dash the pride of this solemnity;
To make his monks and abbots stand like apes,
And point like antics at his triple crown:
To beat the beads about the friars' pates,
Or clap huge horns upon the cardinals' heads:
Or any villainy thou canst devise,
And I'll perform it Faustus: hark, they come:
This day shall make thee be admired in Rome.

Enter the CARDINALS *and Bishops, some bearing croziers, some
the pillars; monks and friars singing their procession.
Then the* POPE *and* RAYMOND *King of Hungary,
with* BRUNO *led in chains*

POPE
Cast down our footstool.
RAYMOND   Saxon Bruno stoop,
Whilst on thy back his holiness ascends
Saint Peter's chair and state pontifical.
BRUNO
Proud Lucifer, that state belongs to me:
But thus I fall to Peter, not to thee.
POPE
To me and Peter, shalt thou grovelling lie,
And crouch before the papal dignity.
Sound trumpets then, for thus Saint Peter's heir,
From Bruno's back ascends Saint Peter's chair.

A flourish while he ascends

Thus, as the gods, creep on with feet of wool,
Long ere with iron hands they punish men,
So shall our sleeping vengeance now arise,
And smite with death thy hated enterprise.
Lord cardinals of France and Padua,
Go forthwith to our holy consistory,
And read amongst the statutes decretal,
What by the holy council held at Trent,
The sacred synod hath decreed for him,
That doth assume the papal government,
Without election, and a true consent:
Away and bring us word with speed.
1 CARDINAL
We go my Lord.   *Exeunt* CARDINALS
POPE
Lord Raymond.

FAUSTUS

Go haste thee, gentle Mephostophilis,
Follow the cardinals to the consistory;
And as they turn their superstitious books,
Strike them with sloth, and drowsy idleness;
And make them sleep so sound, that, in their shapes,
Thyself and I may parley with this pope,
This proud confronter of the emperor;
And in despite of all his holiness
Restore this Bruno to his liberty,
And bear him to the states of Germany.

MEPHOSTOPHILIS

Faustus, I go.

FAUSTUS

Dispatch it soon,
The pope shall curse that Faustus came to Rome.

Exeunt FAUSTUS *and* MEPHOSTOPHILIS

BRUNO

Pope Adrian let me have some right of law,
I was elected by the emperor.

POPE

We will depose the emperor for that deed,
And curse the people that submit to him;
Both he and thou shalt stand excommunicate,
And interdict from church's privilege,
And all society of holy men:
He grows too proud in his authority,
Lifting his lofty head above the clouds,
And like a steeple overpeers the church.
But we'll pull down his haughty insolence:
And as pope Alexander our progenitor,
Trod on the neck of German Frederick,
Adding this golden sentence to our praise:
That Peter's heirs should tread on emperors,
And walk upon the dreadful adder's back,
Treading the lion and the dragon down,
And fearless spurn the killing basilisk:
So will we quell that haughty schismatic,
And by authority apostolical
Depose him from his regal government.

BRUNO

Pope Julius swore to princely Sigismond,
For him, and the succeeding popes of Rome,
To hold the emperors their lawful lords.

POPE

    Pope Julius did abuse the church's rites,
    And therefore none of his decrees can stand.
    Is not all power on earth bestowed on us?
    And therefore tho' we would we cannot err.
    Behold this silver belt whereto is fixed
    Seven golden seals fast sealed with seven seals,
    In token of our seven-fold power from heaven,
    To bind or loose, lock fast, condemn, or judge,
    Resign, or seal, or what so pleaseth us.
    Then he and thou, and all the world shall stoop,
    Or be assured of our dreadful curse,
    To light as heavy as the pains of hell.

Enter FAUSTUS *and* MEPHOSTOPHILIS *like the Cardinals*

MEPHOSTOPHILIS

    Now tell me Faustus, are we not fitted well?

FAUSTUS

    Yes Mephostophilis, and two such cardinals
    Ne'er served a holy pope, as we shall do.
    But whilst they sleep within the consistory,
    Let us salute his reverend fatherhood.

RAYMOND

    Behold my lord, the cardinals are returned.

POPE

    Welcome grave fathers, answer presently,
    What have our holy council there decreed,
    Concerning Bruno and the emperor,
    In quittance of their late conspiracy
    Against our state and papal dignity?

FAUSTUS

    Most sacred patron of the church of Rome,
    By full consent of all the synod
    Of priests and prelates, it is thus decreed:
    That Bruno, and the German emperor
    Be held as lollards, and bold schismatics,
    And proud disturbers of the church's peace.
    And if that Bruno by his own assent,
    Without enforcement of the German peers,
    Did seek to wear the triple diadem,
    And by your death to climb Saint Peter's chair,
    The statutes decretal have thus decreed,
    He shall be straight condemned of heresy,
    And on a pile of faggots burned to death.

POPE

    It is enough. Here, take him to your charge,
    And bear him straight to Ponte Angelo,
    And in the strongest tower enclose him fast.
    Tomorrow, sitting in our consistory,
    With all our college of grave cardinals,
    We will determine of his life or death.
    Here, take his triple crown along with you,
    And leave it in the church's treasury.
    Make haste again, my good lord cardinals,
    And take our blessing apostolical.

MEPHOSTOPHILIS

    So, so, was never devil thus blest before!

FAUSTUS

    Away, sweet Mephostophilis, be gone!
    The cardinals will be plagued for this anon.

                        Exeunt FAUSTUS *and* MEPHOSTOPHILIS

POPE

    Go presently, and bring a banquet forth,
    That we may solemnize Saint Peter's feast,
    And with Lord Raymond, King of Hungary,
    Drink to our late and happy victory.

                                   Exeunt

A sennet while the banquet is brought in; and then enter
  FAUSTUS *and* MEPHOSTOPHILIS *in their own shapes*

MEPHOSTOPHILIS

    Now Faustus, come prepare thyself for mirth;
    The sleepy cardinals are hard at hand,
    To censure Bruno, that is posted hence,
    And on a proud paced steed, as swift as thought,
    Flies o'er the alps to fruitful Germany,
    There to salute the woeful emperor.

FAUSTUS

    The pope will curse them for their sloth today
    That slept both Bruno and his crown away.
    But now, that Faustus may delight his mind,
    And by their folly make some merriment,
    Sweet Mephostophilis, so charm me here,
    That I may walk invisible to all,
    And do whate'er I please, unseen of any.

MEPHOSTOPHILIS

    Faustus thou shalt; then kneel down presently,
    Whilst on thy head I lay my hand,
    And charm thee with this magic wand.

First wear this girdle, then appear
Invisible to all are here:
The planets seven, the gloomy air,
Hell, and the Fury's forked hair,
Pluto's blue fire, and Hecate's tree,
With magic spells so compass thee,
That no eye may thy body see.
So Faustus, now for all their holiness,
Do what thou wilt, thou shalt not be discerned.

FAUSTUS

Thanks Mephostophilis; now friars, take heed
Lest Faustus make your shaven crowns to bleed.

MEPHOSTOPHILIS

Faustus, no more: see where the cardinals come.

Enter POPE *and all the lords. Enter the* CARDINALS
with a book

POPE

Welcome lord cardinals: come sit down.
Lord Raymond, take your seat; friars, attend,
And see that all things be in readiness,
As beseems this solemn festival.

1 CARDINAL

First, may it please your sacred holiness
To view the sentence of the reverend synod,
Concerning Bruno and the emperor.

POPE

What needs this question? Did I not tell you,
Tomorrow we would sit i'th' consistory,
And there determine of his punishment?
You brought us word even now, it was decreed,
That Bruno and the cursed emperor
Were by the holy council both condemned
For loathed lollards, and base schismatics.
Then wherefore would you have me view that book?

1 CARDINAL

Your grace mistakes, you gave us no such charge.

RAYMOND

Deny it not, we are all witnesses
That Bruno here was late delivered you,
With his rich triple crown to be reserved
And put into the church's treasury.

AMBO CARDINALS

By holy Paul we saw them not.

POPE

By Peter you shall die,
Unless you bring them forth immediately:
Hale them to prison, lade their limbs with gyves!
False prelates, for this hateful treachery,
Cursed be your souls to hellish misery.

FAUSTUS

So, they are safe: now Faustus to the feast,
The pope had never such a frolic guest.

POPE

Lord archbishop of Rheims, sit down with us.

BISHOP

I thank your holiness.

FAUSTUS

Fall to, the devil choke you an you spare.

POPE

Who's that spoke? Friars, look about.
Lord Raymond pray fall to; I am beholding
To the bishop of Milan for this so rare a present.

FAUSTUS

I thank you sir.

POPE

How now? Who snatched the meat from me?
Villains, why speak you not?
My good lord archbishop, here's a most dainty dish,
Was sent me from a cardinal in France.

FAUSTUS

I'll have that too.

POPE

What lollards do attend our holiness
That we receive such great indignity? Fetch me some wine.

FAUSTUS

Ay, pray do, for Faustus is a-dry.

POPE

Lord Raymond, I drink unto your grace.

FAUSTUS

I pledge your grace.

POPE

My wine gone too? Ye lubbers, look about
And find the man that doth this villainy,
Or by our sanctitude you all shall die.
I pray my lords, have patience at this
Troublesome banquet.

BISHOP

Please it your holiness, I think it be some ghost crept out of

purgatory, and now is come unto your holiness for his
pardon.

POPE

It may be so:

Go then command our priests to sing a dirge,

To lay the fury of this same troublesome ghost.

FAUSTUS

How now? Must every bit be spiced with a cross?

Nay then, take that.

POPE

O I am slain, help me my lords;

O come and help to bear my body hence.

Damned be this soul for ever, for this deed.

Exeunt the POPE *and his train*

MEPHOSTOPHILIS

Now Faustus, what will you do now? for I can tell you

You'll be cursed with bell, book and candle.

FAUSTUS

Bell, book, and candle; candle, book, and bell:

Forward and backward, to curse Faustus to hell.

Enter the FRIARS *with bell, book, and candle,*
for the dirge

1 FRIAR

Come brethren, let's about our business with good devotion.

Cursed be he that stole his holiness' meat from the table.
Maledicat Dominus.

Cursed be he that struck his holiness a blow [on] the face.
Maledicat Dominus.

Cursed be he that struck friar Sandelo a blow on the pate.
Maledicat Dominus.

Cursed be he that disturbeth our holy dirge.
Maledicat Dominus.

Cursed be he that took away his holiness' wine.
Maledicat Dominus.

Beat the friars, fling fireworks among them,
and exeunt

Exeunt

Scene 8

Enter CLOWN [ROBIN] *and* DICK, *with a cup*

DICK

Sirra Robin, we were best look that your devil can answer
the stealing of this same cup, for the vintner's boy follows
us at the hard heels.

ROBIN

'Tis no matter, let him come; an he follow us, I'll so conjure
him, as he was never conjured in his life, I warrant him. Let
me see the cup.

Enter VINTNER

DICK

Here 'tis. Yonder he comes: now Robin, now or never show
thy cunning.

VINTNER

O, are you here? I am glad I have found you, you are a
couple of fine companions: pray where's the cup you stole
from the tavern?

ROBIN

How, how? We steal a cup? Take heed what you say, we
look not like cup-stealers, I can tell you.

VINTNER

Never deny't, for I know you have it, and I'll search you.

ROBIN

Search me? Ay, and spare not: hold the cup Dick – come,
come, search me, search me.

VINTNER

Come on sirra, let me search you now.

DICK

Ay, ay; do, do. Hold the cup, Robin. I fear not your
searching; we scorn to steal your cups, I can tell you.

VINTNER

Never outface me for the matter, for sure the cup is
between you two.

ROBIN

Nay there you lie, 'tis beyond us both.

VINTNER

A plague take you, I thought 'twas your knavery to take it
away. Come, give it me again.

ROBIN

Ay, much, when can you tell? Dick, make me a circle and

stand close at my back, and stir not for thy life. Vintner, you shall have your cup anon – say nothing, Dick. *O per se o, demogorgon, Belcher* and *Mephostophilis.*

Enter MEPHOSTOPHILIS

MEPHOSTOPHILIS
You princely legions of infernal rule,
How am I vexed by these villains' charms?
From Constantinople have they brought me now,
Only for pleasure of these damned slaves.

ROBIN
By lady sir, you have had a shrewd journey of it! Will it please you to take a shoulder of mutton to supper, and a tester in your purse, and go back again?

DICK
Ay, I pray you heartily sir; for we called you but in jest, I promise you.

MEPHOSTOPHILIS
To purge the rashness of this cursed deed,
First, be thou turned to this ugly shape,
For apish deeds transformed to an ape.

ROBIN
O brave, an ape? I pray sir, let me have the carrying of him about to show some tricks.

MEPHOSTOPHILIS
And so thou shalt: be thou transformed to a dog, and carry him upon thy back. Away, be gone.

ROBIN
A dog? That's excellent: let the maids look well to their porridge-pots, for I'll into the kitchen presently. Come Dick, come.

Exeunt the two CLOWNS

MEPHOSTOPHILIS
Now with the flames of ever-burning fire,
I'll wing my self, and forthwith fly amain
Unto my Faustus, to the great Turk's court.

Exit

Scene 9

Enter MARTINO *and* FREDERICK *at several doors*

MARTINO
What ho, officers, gentlemen,

Hie to the presence to attend the emperor.
Good Frederick, see the rooms be voided straight;
His majesty is coming to the hall;
Go back, and see the state in readiness.

FREDERICK

But where is Bruno, our elected pope,
That on a Fury's back came post from Rome?
Will not his grace consort the emperor?

MARTINO

O yes; and with him comes the German conjuror,
The learned Faustus, fame of Wittenberg,
The wonder of the world for magic art.
And he intends to show great Carolus
The race of all his stout progenitors;
And bring in presence of his majesty
The royal shapes and warlike semblances
Of Alexander and his beauteous paramour.

FREDERICK

Where is Benvolio?

MARTINO

Fast asleep, I warrant you;
He took his rouse with stoops of Rhenish wine
So kindly yesternight to Bruno's health,
That all this day the sluggard keeps his bed.

FREDERICK

See, see – his window's ope; we'll call to him.

MARTINO

What ho, Benvolio!

Enter BENVOLIO *above at a window,*
in his nightcap: buttoning

BENVOLIO

What a devil ail you two?

MARTINO

Speak softly sir, lest the devil hear you:
For Faustus at the court is late arrived,
And at his heels a thousand furies wait
To accomplish whatsoever the doctor please.

BENVOLIO

What of this?

MARTINO

Come, leave thy chamber first, and thou shalt see
This conjuror perform such rare exploits
Before the pope and royal emperor,
As never yet was seen in Germany.

BENVOLIO

Has not the pope enough of conjuring yet?
He was upon the devil's back late enough,
And if he be so far in love with him,
I would he would post with him to Rome again.

FREDERICK

Speak, wilt thou come and see this sport?

BENVOLIO

Not I.

MARTINO

Wilt thou stand in thy window and see it then?

BENVOLIO

Ay, and I fall not asleep i'th' meantime.

MARTINO

The emperor is at hand, who comes to see
What wonders by black spells may compassed be.

BENVOLIO

Well, go you attend the emperor. I am content for this once
to thrust my head out at a window – for they say, if a man
be drunk overnight, the devil cannot hurt him in the
morning. If that be true, I have a charm in my head, shall
control him as well as the conjuror, I warrant you.

[Withdraws]

A sennet. [Enter] CHARLES *the German emperor,* BRUNO,
SAXONY, FAUSTUS, MEPHOSTOPHILIS,
[to]
FREDERICK, MARTINO,
and Attendants

EMPEROR

Wonder of men, renowned magician,
Thrice learned Faustus, welcome to our court.
This deed of thine, in setting Bruno free
From his and our professed enemy,
Shall add more excellence unto thine art
Than if by powerful necromantic spells
Thou couldst command the world's obedience:
For ever be beloved of Carolus.
And if this Bruno thou hast late redeemed
In peace possess the triple diadem,
And sit in Peter's chair, despite of chance,
Thou shalt be famous through all Italy,
And honoured of the German emperor.

FAUSTUS

These gracious words, most royal Carolus,

Shall make poor Faustus to his utmost power
Both love and serve the German emperor,
And lay his life at holy Bruno's feet.
For proof whereof, if so your grace be pleased,
The doctor stands prepared, by power of art,
To cast his magic charms, that shall pierce through
The ebon gates of ever-burning hell,
And hale the stubborn Furies from their caves,
To compass whatso'er your grace commands.

BENVOLIO

'Blood, he speaks terribly! But for all that, I do not greatly believe him: he looks as like conjuror as the pope to a costermonger.

EMPEROR

Then Faustus, as thou late didst promise us,
We would behold that famous conqueror,
Great Alexander, and his paramour,
In their true shapes and state majestical,
That we may wonder at their excellence.

FAUSTUS

Your majesty shall see them presently.
Mephostophilis, away,
And with a solemn noise of trumpets' sound,
Present before this royal emperor,
Great Alexander and his beauteous paramour.

MEPHOSTOPHILIS

Faustus I will.

BENVOLIO

Well master doctor, an your devils come not away quickly, you shall have me asleep presently: zounds, I could eat myself for anger, to think I have been such an ass all this while, to stand gaping after the devil's governor, and can see nothing.

FAUSTUS

I'll make you feel something anon, if my art fail me not.
My lord, I must forewarn your majesty
That when my spirits present the royal shapes
Of Alexander and his paramour,
Your grace demand no questions of the king,
But in dumb silence let them come and go.

EMPEROR

Be it as Faustus please, we are content.

BENVOLIO

Ay, ay; and I am content too: and thou bring Alexander and his paramour before the emperor, I'll be Actaeon, and turn myself into a stag.

FAUSTUS
And I'll play Diana, and send you the horns presently.

Sennet. Enter at one [door] the emperor ALEXANDER, *at
the other [door]* DARIUS; *they meet,* DARIUS *is thrown
down,* ALEXANDER *kills him, takes off his crown,
and offering to go out, his paramour meets him. He embraceth
her, and sets Darius' crown upon her head; and coming
back, both salute the emperor who, leaving his state, offers to
embrace them, which* FAUSTUS *seeing, suddenly stays him.
Then trumpets cease, and music sounds*

My gracious lord, you do forget yourself:
These are but shadows, not substantial.
EMPEROR
O pardon me, my thoughts are so ravished
With sight of this renowned emperor,
That in mine arms I would have compassed him.
But Faustus, since I may not speak to them,
To satisfy my longing thoughts at full,
Let me this tell thee: I have heard it said,
That this fair lady, whilst she lived on earth,
Had on her neck a little wart or mole;
How may I prove that saying to be true?
FAUSTUS
Your majesty may boldly go and see.
EMPEROR
Faustus, I see it plain!
And in this sight thou better pleasest me,
Than if I gained another monarchy.
FAUSTUS
Away, be gone.   *Exit Show*
See, see, my gracious lord, what strange beast is yon, that
thrusts his head out at window.
EMPEROR
O wondrous sight: see, duke of Saxony,
Two spreading horns most strangely fastened
Upon the head of young Benvolio.
SAXONY
What, is he asleep – or dead?
FAUSTUS
He sleeps, my lord, but dreams not of his horns.
EMPEROR
This sport is excellent: we'll call and wake him.
What ho, Benvolio!

BENVOLIO

A plague upon you, let me sleep awhile.

EMPEROR

I blame thee not to sleep much, having such a head of thine own.

SAXONY

Look up, Benvolio; 'tis the emperor calls.

BENVOLIO

The emperor! Where? O zounds, my head.

EMPEROR

Nay, and thy horns hold, 'tis no matter for thy head, for that's armed sufficiently.

FAUSTUS

Why, how now sir knight, what hanged by the horns? This [is] most horrible: fie, fie, pull in your head for shame, let not all the world wonder at you.

BENVOLIO

Zounds, doctor, is this your villainy?

FAUSTUS

O say not so, sir: the doctor has no skill,
No art, no cunning, to present these lords,
Or bring before this royal emperor
The mighty monarch, warlike Alexander.
If Faustus do it, you are straight resolved
In bold Actaeon's shape to turn a stag.
And therefore, my lord – so please your majesty –
I'll raise a kennel of hounds shall hunt him so
As all his footmanship shall scarce prevail
To keep his carcass from their bloody fangs.
Ho, Belimoth, Argiron, Asteroth!

BENVOLIO

Hold, hold! Zounds, he'll raise up a kennel of devils, I think, anon. Good my lord, entreat for me: 'sblood, I am never able to endure these torments.

EMPEROR

Then, good master doctor,
Let me entreat you to remove his horns:
He has done penance now sufficiently.

FAUSTUS

My gracious lord, not so much for injury done to me, as to delight your majesty with some mirth, hath Faustus justly requited this injurious knight; which being all I desire, I am content to remove his horns. Mephostophilis, transform him; and hereafter sir, look you speak well of scholars.

BENVOLIO

Speak well of you? 'Sblood, and scholars be such cuckold-
makers to clap horns of honest men's heads o'this order, I'll
ne'er trust smooth faces and small ruffs more. But an I be
not revenged for this, would I might be turned to a gaping
oyster and drink nothing but salt water.   [*Exit*]

EMPEROR

Come Faustus; while the emperor lives,
In recompence of this thy high desert,
Thou shalt command the state of Germany,
And live beloved of mighty Carolus.

Exeunt omnes

Enter BENVOLIO, MARTINO, FREDERICK,
and Soldiers

MARTINO

Nay, sweet Benvolio, let us sway thy thoughts
From this attempt against the conjuror.

BENVOLIO

Away, you love me not to urge me thus.
Shall I let slip so great an injury,
When every servile groom jests at my wrongs,
And in their rustic gambols proudly say,
'Benvolio's head was graced with horns today'!
O may these eyelids never close again,
Till with my sword I have that conjuror slain.
If you will aid me in this enterprise,
Then draw your weapons, and be resolute:
If not, depart: here will Benvolio die –
But Faustus' death shall quit my infamy!

FREDERICK

Nay, we will stay with thee, betide what may,
And kill that doctor if he come this way.

BENVOLIO

Then gentle Frederick, hie thee to the grove,
And place our servants, and our followers
Close in an ambush there behind the trees;
By this (I know) the conjuror is near:
I saw him kneel, and kiss the emperor's hand,
And take his leave, laden with rich rewards.
Then soldiers, boldly fight; if Faustus die,
Take you the wealth, leave us the victory.

FREDERICK

Come soldiers, follow me unto the grove;
Who kills him shall have gold, and endless love.

Exit FREDERICK *with the* SOLDIERS

BENVOLIO

My head is lighter than it was by th'horns,
But yet my heart more ponderous than my head,
And pants until I see that conjuror dead.

MARTINO

Where shall we place ourselves Benvolio?

BENVOLIO

Here will we stay to bide the first assault.
O were that damned hellhound but in place,
Thou soon shouldst see me quit my foul disgrace.

Enter FREDERICK

FREDERICK

Close, close, the conjuror is at hand,
And, all alone, comes walking in his gown.
Be ready then, and strike the peasant down.

BENVOLIO

Mine be that honour then: now sword strike home,
For horns he gave, I'll have his head anon.

Enter FAUSTUS *with the false head*

MARTINO

See, see, he comes.

BENVOLIO

No words: this blow ends all!
Hell take his soul, his body thus must fall.

FAUSTUS

Oh.

FREDERICK

Groan you, master doctor?

BENVOLIO

Break may his heart with groans! Dear Frederick, see
Thus will I end his griefs immediately.

MARTINO

Strike with a willing hand, his head is off.

BENVOLIO

The devil's dead, the furies now may laugh.

FREDERICK

Was this that stern aspect, that awful frown,
Made the grim monarch of infernal spirits
Tremble and quake at his commanding charms?

MARTINO

Was this that damned head, whose heart conspired
Benvolio's shame before the emperor?

BENVOLIO
  Ay, that's the head, and here the body lies,
  Justly rewarded for his villainies.
FREDERICK
  Come, let's devise how we may add more shame
  To the black scandal of his hated name.
BENVOLIO
  First, on his head, in quittance of my wrongs,
  I'll nail huge forked horns, and let them hang
  Within the window where he yoked me first,
  That all the world may see my just revenge.
MARTINO
  What use shall we put his beard to?
BENVOLIO
  We'll sell it to a chimney-sweeper: it will wear out ten
  birchen brooms, I warrant you.
FREDERICK
  What shall eyes do?
BENVOLIO
  We'll put out his eyes, and they shall serve for buttons to
  his lips, to keep his tongue from catching cold.
MARTINO
  An excellent policy! And now sirs, having divided him,
  what shall the body do?

                                        [FAUSTUS *gets up*]

BENVOLIO
  Zounds, the devil's alive again.
FREDERICK
  Give him his head, for God's sake.
FAUSTUS
  Nay keep it: Faustus will have heads and hands,
  Ay, all your hearts to recompense this deed.
  Knew you not, traitors, I was limited
  For four-and-twenty years to breathe on earth?
  And had you cut my body with your swords,
  Or hew'd this flesh and bones as small as sand,
  Yet in a minute had my spirit returned,
  And I had breathed a man made free from harm.
  But wherefore do I dally my revenge?
  Asteroth, Belimoth, Mephostophilis.

          Enter MEPHOSTOPHILIS *and other* DEVILS

  Go, horse these traitors on your fiery backs,
  And mount aloft with them as high as heaven,
  Thence pitch them headlong to the lowest hell:

Yet stay, the world shall see their misery,
And hell shall after plague their treachery.
Go Belimoth, and take this caitiff hence,
And hurl him in some lake of mud and dirt;
Take thou this other, drag him through the woods,
Amongst the pricking thorns and sharpest briars,
Whilst with my gentle Mephostophilis,
This traitor flies unto some steepy rock,
That rolling down, may break the villain's bones,
As he intended to dismember me.
Fly hence, dispatch my charge immediately.

FREDERICK
Pity us, gentle Faustus, save our lives.

FAUSTUS
Away.

FREDERICK
He must needs go that the devil drives.

Exeunt SPIRITS *with the* KNIGHTS

Enter the ambushed SOLDIERS

1 SOLDIER
Come sirs, prepare yourselves in readiness,
Make haste to help these noble gentlemen.
I heard them parley with the conjuror.

2 SOLDIER
See where he comes! Dispatch, and kill the slave.

FAUSTUS
What's here? An ambush to betray my life!
Then Faustus, try thy skill: base peasants stand,
For lo, these trees remove at my command,
And stand as bulwarks 'twixt yourselves and me,
To shield me from your hated treachery!
Yet to encounter this your weak attempt,
Behold an army comes incontinent.

FAUSTUS *strikes the door, and enter a* DEVIL *playing
on a drum; after him another bearing an ensign; and
divers with weapons;* MEPHOSTOPHILIS *with fireworks.
They set upon the* SOLDIERS, *and drive them out*

Enter at several doors BENVOLIO, FREDERICK, *and* MARTINO,
*their heads and faces bloody, and besmeared with
mud and dirt; all having horns on their heads*

MARTINO
What ho, Benvolio!

BENVOLIO

Here, what Frederick, ho!

FREDERICK

O help me, gentle friend; where is Martino?

MARTINO

Dear Frederick, here –

Half smothered in a lake of mud and dirt,

Through which the Furies dragged me by the heels.

FREDERICK

Martino, see

Benvolio's horns again!

MARTINO

O misery! How now Benvolio?

BENVOLIO

Defend me heaven, shall I be haunted still?

MARTINO

Nay fear not, man; we have no power to kill.

BENVOLIO

My friends transformed thus: O hellish spite,

Your heads are all set with horns.

FREDERICK   You hit it right,

It is your own you mean: feel on your head.

BENVOLIO

'Zounds, horns again!

MARTINO

Nay chafe not, man: we all are sped.

BENVOLIO

What devil attends this damned magician,

That spite of spite our wrongs are doubled?

FREDERICK

What may we do, that we may hide our shames?

BENVOLIO

If we should follow him to work revenge,

He'd join long asses' ears to these huge horns,

And make us laughing-stocks to all the world.

MARTINO

What shall we do then, dear Benvolio?

BENVOLIO

I have a castle joining near these woods,

And thither we'll repair, and live obscure

Till time shall alter this our brutish shapes.

Sith black disgrace hath thus eclipsed our fame,

We'll rather die with grief, than live with shame.

            Exeunt omnes

Scene 10

Enter FAUSTUS *and the* HORSE-COURSER,
and MEPHOSTOPHILIS

HORSE-COURSER
I beseech your worship accept of these forty dollars.
FAUSTUS
Friend, thou canst not buy so good a horse, for so small a
price: I have no great need to sell him, but if thou likest him
for ten dollars more, take him, because I see thou hast a
good mind to him.
HORSE-COURSER
I beseech you sir, accept of this; I am a very poor man, and
have lost very much of late by horseflesh, and this bargain
will set me up again.
FAUSTUS
Well, I will not stand with thee; give me the money. Now
sirra I must tell you, that you may ride him o'er hedge and
ditch, and spare him not; but, do you hear, in any case ride
him not into the water.
HORSE-COURSER
How sir, not into the water? Why, will he not drink of all
waters?
FAUSTUS
Yes, he will drink of all waters, but ride him not into the
water: o'er hedge and ditch, or where thou wilt, but not into
the water. Go bid the ostler deliver him unto you, and
remember what I say.
HORSE-COURSER
I warrant you sir. O joyful day! Now am I a made man for
ever.

Exit

FAUSTUS
What art thou, Faustus, but a man condemned to die?
Thy fatal time draws to a final end;
Despair doth drive distrust into my thoughts.
Confound these passions with a quiet sleep:
Tush, Christ did call the thief upon the cross,
Then rest thee, Faustus, quiet in conceit.

He sits to sleep

Enter the HORSE-COURSER *wet*

HORSE-COURSER

> O what a cozening doctor was this! I riding my horse into
> the water, thinking some hidden mystery had been in the
> horse, I had nothing under me but a little straw, and had
> much ado to escape drowning! Well, I'll go rouse him, and
> make him give me my forty dollars again. Ho, sirra doctor,
> you cozening scab; master doctor awake, and rise, and give
> me my money again, for your horse is turned to a bottle of
> hay, – master doctor.

He pulls off his leg

> Alas I am undone, what shall I do? I have pulled off his leg.

FAUSTUS

> O help, help, the villain hath murdered me.

HORSE-COURSER

> Murder or not murder, now he has but one leg, I'll out-run
> him, and cast this leg into some ditch or other.

Exit

FAUSTUS

> Stop him, stop him, stop him – ha, ha, ha, Faustus hath his
> leg again, and the horse-courser a bundle of hay for his
> forty dollars.

Enter WAGNER

> How now Wagner, what news with thee?

WAGNER

> If it please you, the Duke of Vanholt doth earnestly entreat
> your company, and hath sent some of his men to attend you
> with provision fit for your journey.

FAUSTUS

> The Duke of Vanholt's an honourable gentleman, and one
> to whom I must be no niggard of my cunning. Come away.

Exeunt

Scene 10b

[This scene is found only the B Text, where it is inserted
after Wagner's announcement of the Duke of Vanholt's
invitation.]

Enter CLOWN [ROBIN], DICK, HORSE-COURSER *and a*
CARTER

CARTER

> Come, my masters, I'll bring you to the best beer in Europe.
> What ho, hostess, where be these whores?

Enter HOSTESS

HOSTESS
How now, what lack you? What, my old guests, welcome.
ROBIN
Sirra Dick, dost thou know why I stand so mute?
DICK
No Robin, why is't?
ROBIN
I am eighteen pence on the score, but say nothing, see if she have forgotten me.
HOSTESS
Who's this, that stands so solemnly by himself? What, my old guest?
ROBIN
O hostess, how do you? I hope my score stands still.
HOSTESS
Ay, there's no doubt of that, for methinks you make no haste to wipe it out.
DICK
Why hostess, I say, fetch us some beer.
HOSTESS
You shall presently: look up into th'hall there, ho!

Exit

DICK
Come sirs, what shall we do now till mine hostess comes?
CARTER
Marry sir, I'll tell you the bravest tale how a conjuror served me; you know Doctor Fauster?
HORSE-COURSER
Ay, a plague take him! Here's some on's have cause to know him; did he conjure thee too?
CARTER
I'll tell you how he served me. As I was going to Wittenberg t'other day, with a load of hay, he met me, and asked me what he should give me for as much hay as he could eat; now sir, I thinking that a little would serve his turn, bade him take as much as he would for three-farthings; so he presently gave me my money, and fell to eating; and as I am a christen man, he never left eating, till he had ate up all my load of hay.
ALL
O monstrous, eat a whole load of hay!
ROBIN
Yes, yes, that may be; for I have heard of one, that ha's ate a load of logs.

HORSE-COURSER

Now sirs, you shall hear how villainously he served me: I went to him yesterday to buy a horse of him, and he would by no means sell him under forty dollars; so sir, because I knew him to be such a horse, as would run over hedge and ditch, and never tire, I gave him his money; so when I had my horse, Doctor Fauster bade me ride him night and day, and spare him no time; but, quoth he, in any case ride him not into the water. Now sir, I thinking the horse had had some quality that he would not have me know of, what did I but rid him into a great river, and when I came just in the midst my horse vanished away, and I sat straddling upon a bottle of hay.

ALL

O brave, doctor!

HORSE-COURSER

But you shall hear how bravely I served him for it. I went me home to his house, and there I found him asleep. I kept a hallowing and whooping in his ears, but all could not wake him: I, seeing that, took him by the leg, and never rested pulling, till I had pulled me his leg quite off, and now 'tis at home in mine hostry.

ROBIN

And has the doctor but one leg then? That's excellent, for one of his devils turned me into the likeness of an ape's face.

CARTER

Some more drink, hostess.

ROBIN

Hark you, we'll into another room and drink awhile, and then we'll go seek out the doctor.

Exeunt omnes

Scene 11

Enter the DUKE *of Vanholt; his* DUCHESS,
FAUSTUS, *and* MEPHOSTOPHILIS

DUKE

Thanks, master doctor, for these pleasant sights; nor know I how sufficiently to recompense your great deserts in erecting that enchanted castle in the air; the sight whereof so delighted me, as nothing in the world could please me more.

FAUSTUS

I do think myself, my good lord, highly recompensed, in
that it pleaseth your grace to think but well of that which
Faustus hath performed. But, gracious lady, it may be, that
you have taken no pleasure in those sights; therefore I pray
you tell me, what is the thing you most desire to have: be it
in the world, it shall be yours. I have heard that great-
bellied women do long for things are rare and dainty.

DUCHESS

True, master doctor; and since I find you so kind I will
make known unto you what my heart desires to have; and
were it now summer, as it is January, a dead time of the
winter, I would request no better meat, than a dish of ripe
grapes.

FAUSTUS

This is but a small matter: go Mephostophilis; away!

Exit MEPHOSTOPHILIS

Madam, I will do more than this for your content.

Enter MEPHOSTOPHILIS *again with the grapes*

Here, now taste ye these: they should be good
For they come from a far country, I can tell you.

DUKE

This makes me wonder more than all the rest, that at this
time of the year, when every tree is barren of his fruit, from
whence you had these ripe grapes.

FAUSTUS

Please it your grace, the year is divided into two circles
over the whole world, so that when it is winter with us, in
the contrary circle it is likewise summer with them, as in
India, Saba, and such countries that lie far east, where they
have fruit twice a year. From whence, by means of a swift
spirit that I have, I had these grapes brought as you see.

DUCHESS

And trust me, they are the sweetest grapes that e'er I tasted.

The CLOWNS [ROBIN, DICK, CARTER, HORSE-COURSER]
bounce at the gate, within

DUKE

What rude disturbers have we at the gate?
Go pacify their fury, set it ope,
And then demand of them, what they would have.

They knock again, and call out to talk with FAUSTUS
[*within*]

A SERVANT
Why how now masters, what a coil is there?
What is the reason you disturb the duke?
DICK
We have no reason for it, therefore a fig for him.
SERVANT
Why saucy varlets, dare you be so bold?
HORSE-COURSER
I hope sir, we have wit enough to be more bold than
welcome.
SERVANT
It appears so. Pray be bold elsewhere,
And trouble not the duke.
DUKE
What would they have?
SERVANT
They all cry out to speak with Doctor Faustus.
CARTER
Ay, and we will speak with him.
DUKE
Will you sir? Commit the rascals.
DICK
Commit with us! He were as good commit with his father,
as commit with us.
FAUSTUS
I do beseech your grace let them come in,
They are good subject for a merriment.
DUKE
Do as thou wilt Faustus, I give thee leave.
FAUSTUS
I thank your grace:

Enter [ROBIN], DICK, CARTER, *and* HORSE-COURSER

Why, how now, my good friends?
'Faith you are too outrageous, but come near,
I have procured your pardons: welcome all.
ROBIN
Nay sir, we will be welcome for our money, and we will pay
for what we take. What ho, give's half a dozen of beer here,
and be hanged.
FAUSTUS
Nay, hark you, can you tell me where you are?
CARTER
Ay, marry can I, we are under heaven.

SERVANT

Ay; but, sir sauce-box, know you in what place?

HORSE-COURSER

Ay, ay: the house is good enough to drink in. Zounds, fill us some beer, or we'll break all the barrels in the house, and dash out all your brains with your bottles.

FAUSTUS

Be not so furious: come, you shall have beer.

My Lord, beseech you give me leave awhile,

I'll gage my credit, 'twill content your grace.

DUKE

With all my heart, kind doctor; please thyself,

Our servants, and our court's at thy command.

FAUSTUS

I humbly thank your grace: then fetch some beer.

HORSE-COURSER

Ay, marry; there spake a doctor indeed – and 'faith I'll drink a health to thy wooden leg for that word.

FAUSTUS

My wooden leg? what dost thou mean by that?

CARTER

Ha, ha, ha, dost hear him Dick? He has forgot his leg.

HORSE-COURSER

Ay, ay, he does not stand much upon that.

FAUSTUS

No 'faith, not much upon a wooden leg.

CARTER

Good Lord, that flesh and blood should be so frail with your worship! Do not you remember a horse-courser you sold a horse to?

FAUSTUS

Yes, I remember I sold one a horse.

CARTER

And do you remember you bid he should not ride into the water?

FAUSTUS

Yes, I do very well remember that.

CARTER

And do you remember nothing of your leg?

FAUSTUS

No, in good sooth.

CARTER

Then I pray remember your courtesy.

FAUSTUS [*bowing*]

I thank you sir.

CARTER

'Tis not so much worth; I pray you tell me one thing.

FAUSTUS

What's that?

CARTER

Be both your legs bedfellows every night together?

FAUSTUS

Wouldst thou make a colossus of me, that thou askest me such questions?

CARTER

No, truly sir, I would make nothing of you, but I would fain know that.

Enter HOSTESS *with drink*

FAUSTUS

Then I assure thee certainly they are.

CARTER

I thank you; I am fully satisfied.

FAUSTUS

But wherefore dost thou ask?

CARTER

For nothing sir: but methinks you should have a wooden bedfellow of one of 'em.

HORSE-COURSER

Why, do you hear sir, did not I pull off one of your legs when you were asleep?

FAUSTUS

But I have it again now I am awake: look you here, sir.

ALL

O horrible! Had the doctor three legs?

CARTER

Do you remember sir, how you cozened me and eat up my load of –

FAUSTUS *charms him dumb*

DICK

Do you remember how you made me wear an ape's –

HORSE-COURSER

You whoreson conjuring scab, do you remember how you cozened me with a ho –

ROBIN

Ha' you forgotten me? You think to carry it away with your hey-pass and re-pass: do you remember the dog's fa –

Exeunt CLOWNS

HOSTESS

Who pays for the ale – hear you, master doctor, now you

have sent away my guests. I pray who shall pay me for my
a –

Exit HOSTESS

DUCHESS
My lord,
We are much beholding to this learned man.
DUKE
So are we madam, which we will recompense
With all the love and kindness that we may:
His artful sport drives all sad thoughts away.

Exeunt

Scene 12

Thunder and lightning. Enter DEVILS *with covered dishes;*
MEPHOSTOPHILIS *leads them into* FAUSTUS' *study*
Then enter WAGNER

WAGNER
I think my master means to die shortly. He has made his
will, and given me his wealth, his house, his goods, and
store of golden plate, besides two thousand ducats ready
coined: I wonder what he means? If death were nigh, he
would not frolic thus: he's now at supper with the scholars,
where there's such belly-cheer, as Wagner in his life ne'er
saw the like! And see where they come, belike the feast is
done.

Exit

Enter FAUSTUS, MEPHOSTOPHILIS, *and two or three*
SCHOLARS

1 SCHOLAR
Master doctor Faustus, since our conference about fair
ladies, which was the beautifullest in all the world, we have
determined with ourselves, that Helen of Greece was the
admirablest lady that ever lived: therefore master doctor, if
you will do us so much favour, as to let us see that peerless
dame of Greece, whom all the world admires for majesty,
we should think ourselves much beholding unto you.
FAUSTUS
Gentlemen, for that I know your friendship is unfained,
It is not Faustus' custom to deny
The just request of those that wish him well:
You shall behold that peerless dame of Greece,

No otherwise for pomp or majesty,
Than when sir Paris crossed the seas with her,
And brought the spoils to rich Dardania.
Be silent then, for danger is in words.

Music sound. MEPHOSTOPHILIS *brings in* HELEN;
she passeth over the stage

2 SCHOLAR
Was this fair Helen, whose admired worth
Made Greece with ten years' war afflict poor Troy?
3 SCHOLAR
Too simple is my wit to tell her worth,
Whom all the world admires for majesty.
1 SCHOLAR
Now we have seen the pride of Nature's work,
We'll take our leaves, and for this blessed sight
Happy and blest be Faustus evermore.
                                      Exeunt SCHOLARS
FAUSTUS
Gentlemen farewell: the same wish I to you.

Enter an OLD MAN

OLD MAN
O gentle Faustus, leave this damned art,
This magic, that will charm thy soul to hell,
And quite bereave thee of salvation.
Though thou hast now offended like a man,
Do not persevere in it like a devil.
Yet, yet, thou hast an amiable soul,
If sin by custom grow not into nature.
Then Faustus, will repentance come too late,
Then thou art banished from the sight of heaven.
No mortal can express the pains of hell!
It may be this my exhortation
Seems harsh, and all unpleasant; let it not,
For, gentle son, I speak it not in wrath,
Or envy of thee, but in tender love,
And pity of thy future misery.
And so have hope, that this my kind rebuke,
Checking thy body, may amend thy soul.
FAUSTUS
Where art thou, Faustus? wretch, what hast thou done?
Hell claims his right, and with a roaring voice,
                    MEPHOSTOPHILIS *gives him a dagger*
Says 'Faustus, come: thine hour is almost come';

And Faustus now will come to do thee right.

OLD MAN

O stay, good Faustus, stay thy desperate steps.
I see an angel hover o'er thy head,
And with a vial full of precious grace,
Offers to pour the same into thy soul!
Then call for mercy, and avoid despair.

FAUSTUS

O friend, I feel thy words to comfort my distressed soul!
Leave me awhile, to ponder on my sins.

OLD MAN

Faustus I leave thee, but with grief of heart,
Fearing the enemy of thy hapless soul.　　　　　　　*Exit*

FAUSTUS

Accursed Faustus, wretch, what hast thou done?
I do repent, and yet I do despair,
Hell strives with grace for conquest in my breast:
What shall I do to shun the snares of death?

MEPHOSTOPHILIS

Thou traitor Faustus, I arrest thy soul
For disobedience to my sovereign lord.
Revolt, or I'll in piecemeal tear thy flesh...

[From this point the two texts coincide, except that B omits
the final appearance (and speech) of the Old Man.]

Scene 13

Thunder. Enter LUCIFER, BELZEBUB, *and* MEPHOSTOPHILIS

LUCIFER

Thus from infernal Dis do we ascend
To view the subjects of our monarchy,
Those souls which sin seals the black sons of hell.
'Mong which as chief, Faustus, we come to thee,
Bringing with us lasting damnation
To wait upon thy soul; the time is come
Which makes it forfeit.

MEPHOSTOPHILIS　　　　　　And this gloomy night,
Here in this room will wretched Faustus be.

BELZEBUB

And here we'll stay,
To mark him how he doth demean himself.

MEPHOSTOPHILIS
　　How should he, but in desperate lunacy.
　　Fond worldling, now his heart-blood dries with grief;
　　His conscience kills it, and his labouring brain
　　Begets a world of idle fantasies,
　　To overreach the devil. But all in vain:
　　His store of pleasures must be sauced with pain.
　　He and his servant Wagner are at hand,
　　Both come from drawing Faustus' latest will.
　　See where they come.

Enter FAUSTUS *and* WAGNER

FAUSTUS
　　Say, Wagner, thou hast perused my will,
　　How dost thou like it?
WAGNER　　　　　　　　Sir, so wondrous well,
　　As in all humble duty, I do yield
　　My life and lasting service for your love.

Enter the SCHOLARS

FAUSTUS
　　Gramercies Wagner. Welcome gentlemen.
1 SCHOLAR
　　Now worthy Faustus, methinks your looks are changed.
FAUSTUS
　　O gentlemen!
2 SCHOLAR
　　What ails Faustus?
FAUSTUS
　　Ah my sweet chamber-fellow, had I lived with thee,
　　Then had I lived still, but now must die eternally.
　　Look sirs, comes he not, comes he not?
1 SCHOLAR
　　O my dear Faustus, what imports this fear?
2 SCHOLAR
　　Is all our pleasure turned to melancholy?
3 SCHOLAR
　　He is not well with being over-solitary.
2 SCHOLAR
　　If it be so, we'll have physicians, and Faustus shall
　　be cured.
3 SCHOLAR
　　'Tis but a surfeit sir, fear nothing.

FAUSTUS

A surfeit of deadly sin, that hath damned both body and soul.

3 SCHOLAR

Yet Faustus, look up to heaven, and remember mercy is infinite.

FAUSTUS

But Faustus' offence can ne'er be pardoned!
The serpent that tempted Eve may be saved,
But not Faustus. O gentlemen, hear with patience, and tremble not at my speeches, though my heart pant and quiver to remember that I have been a student here these thirty years – O would I had never seen Wittenberg, never read book; and what wonders I have done, all Germany can witness – yea, all the world – for which Faustus hath lost both Germany and the world – yea, heaven itself, heaven, the seat of God, the throne of the blessed, the kingdom of joy; and must remain in hell for ever. Hell, O hell for ever. Sweet friends, what shall become of Faustus being in hell for ever?

2 SCHOLAR

Yet Faustus call on God.

FAUSTUS

On God, whom Faustus hath abjured? On God, whom Faustus hath blasphemed! O my God, I would weep, but the devil draws in my tears. Gush forth blood instead of tears, yea life and soul: O, he stays my tongue: I would lift up my hands, but see they hold 'em, they hold 'em.

ALL

Who Faustus?

FAUSTUS

Why, Lucifer and Mephostophilis!
O gentlemen, I gave them my soul for my cunning.

ALL

O God forbid.

FAUSTUS

God forbade it indeed, but Faustus hath done it: for the vain pleasure of four-and-twenty years hath Faustus lost eternal joy and felicity. I writ them a bill with mine own blood, the date is expired: this is the time, and he will fetch me.

1 SCHOLAR

Why did not Faustus tell us of this before, that divines might have prayed for thee?

FAUSTUS

Oft have I thought to have done so: but the devil threatened
to tear me in pieces if I named God: to fetch me body and
soul, if I once gave ear to divinity: and now 'tis too late.
Gentlemen away, lest you perish with me.

2 SCHOLAR

O what may we do to save Faustus?

FAUSTUS

Talk not of me, but save yourselves and depart.

3 SCHOLAR

God will strengthen me; I will stay with Faustus.

1 SCHOLAR

Tempt not God, sweet friend, but let us into the next room,
and pray for him.

FAUSTUS

Ay, pray for me, pray for me: and what noise soever you
hear, come not unto me, for nothing can rescue me.

2 SCHOLAR

Pray thou, and we will pray, that God may have mercy
upon thee.

FAUSTUS

Gentlemen farewell. If I live till morning, I'll visit you: if
not, Faustus is gone to hell.

ALL

Faustus, farewell.

Exeunt SCHOLARS

MEPHOSTOPHILIS

Ay, Faustus, now thou hast no hope of heaven,
Therefore despair, think only upon hell;
For that must be thy mansion, there to dwell.

FAUSTUS

O thou bewitching fiend, 'twas thy temptation
Hath robbed me of eternal happiness.

MEPHOSTOPHILIS

I do confess it Faustus, and rejoice!
'Twas I, that when thou wer't i'the way to heaven,
Dam'd up thy passage; when thou took'st the book
To view the Scriptures, then I turned the leaves
And led thine eye.
What weep'st thou? 'Tis too late; despair; farewell.
Fools that will laugh on earth, must weep in hell.

Exit

Enter the GOOD ANGEL *and the* BAD ANGEL
at several doors

GOOD ANGEL

O Faustus, if thou hadst given ear to me,
Innumerable joys had followed thee.
But thou didst love the world.

BAD ANGEL   Gave ear to me,
And now must taste hell's pains perpetually.

GOOD ANGEL

O what will all thy riches, pleasures, pomps,
Avail thee now?

BAD ANGEL   Nothing but vex thee more,
To want in hell, that had on earth such store.

Music while the throne descends

GOOD ANGEL

O thou has lost celestial happiness,
Pleasures unspeakable, bliss without end.
Hadst thou affected sweet divinity,
Hell, or the devil, had had no power on thee.
Hadst thou kept on that way, Faustus behold,
In what resplendent glory thou hadst sat
In yonder throne, like those bright shining saints,
And triumphed over hell: that hast thou lost,
And now poor soul must thy good angel leave thee,
The jaws of hell are open to receive thee.

                                             Exit

Hell is discovered

BAD ANGEL

Now Faustus, let thine eyes with horror stare
Into that vast perpetual torture-house.
There are the Furies tossing damned souls,
On burning forks; there, bodies boil in lead.
There are live quarters broiling on the coals,
That ne'er can die! This ever-burning chair
Is for o'er-tortured souls to rest them in.
These, that are fed with sops of flaming fire,
Were gluttons, and loved only delicates,
And laughed to see the poor starve at their gates.
But yet all these are nothing. Thou shalt see
Ten thousand tortures that more horrid be.

FAUSTUS

O, I have seen enough to torture me.

BAD ANGEL

Nay, thou must feel them, taste the smart of all.
He that loves pleasure, must for pleasure fall:

And so I leave thee Faustus till anon,
Then wilt thou tumble in confusion.

Exit

The clock strikes eleven

FAUSTUS
    O Faustus,
    Now hast thou but one bare hour to live,
    And then thou must be damned perpetually.
    Stand still, you ever moving spheres of heaven,
    That time may cease, and midnight never come.
    Fair Nature's eye, rise, rise again and make
    Perpetual day: or let this hour be but a year,
    A month, a week, a natural day,
    That Faustus may repent, and save his soul.
    O lente lente currite noctis equi!
    The stars move still, time runs, the clock will strike.
    The devil will come, and Faustus must be damned.
    O I'll leap up to heaven: who pulls me down?
    One drop of blood will save me; O my Christ,
    Rend not my heart for naming of my Christ.
    Yet will I call on him: O spare me Lucifer.
    Where is it now? 'Tis gone.
    And see a threatening arm, an angry brow.
    Mountains and hills, come, come, and fall on me,
    And hide me from the heavy wrath of heaven.
    No? Then will I headlong run into the earth:
    Gape earth! O no, it will not harbour me.
    You stars that reigned at my nativity,
    Whose influence hath allotted death and hell,
    Now draw up Faustus like a foggy mist,
    Into the entrails of yon labouring cloud,
    That when you vomit forth into the air,
    My limbs may issue from your smoky mouths,
    But let my soul mount, and ascend to heaven.

The watch strikes

O half the hour is past: 'twill all be past anon!
O, if my soul must suffer for my sin,
Impose some end to my incessant pain!
Let Faustus live in hell a thousand years,
A hundred thousand, and at last be saved.
No end is limited to damned souls.
Why wert thou not a creature wanting soul?
Or why is this immortal that thou hast?

O Pythagoras' *metempsychosis* – were that true,
This soul should fly from me, and I be changed
Into some brutish beast.
All beasts are happy, for when they die,
Their souls are soon dissolved in elements,
But mine must live still to be plagued in hell.
Cursed be the parents that engendered me;
No Faustus, curse thyself, curse Lucifer,
That hath deprived thee of the joys of heaven.

The clock strikes twelve

It strikes, it strikes! Now body, turn to air,
Or Lucifer will bear thee quick to hell.
O soul be changed into small water drops,
And fall into the ocean, ne'er be found.

Thunder, and enter the DEVILS

O mercy heaven, look not so fierce on me;
Adders and serpents, let me breathe awhile!
Ugly hell, gape not! Come not Lucifer!
I'll burn my books! O Mephostophilis!

Exeunt

[An additional scene, inserted between the final soliloquy
and the Epilogue.]

Scene 13+

Enter the SCHOLARS

1 SCHOLAR
Come gentlemen, let us go visit Faustus,
For such a dreadful night was never seen
Since first the world's creation did begin.
Such fearful shrieks and cries were never heard!
Pray heaven the doctor have escaped the danger.
2 SCHOLAR
O help us heaven! See, here are Faustus' limbs,
All torn asunder by the hand of death.
3 SCHOLAR
The devils whom Faustus served have torn him thus!
For 'twixt the hours of twelve and one, methought
I heard him shriek and call aloud for help:

At which self time the house seemed all on fire
With dreadful horror of these damned fiends.
2 SCHOLAR
Well gentlemen, tho' Faustus' end be such
As every Christian heart laments to think on,
Yet, for he was a scholar, once admired
For wondrous knowledge in our German schools,
We'll give his mangled limbs due burial.
And all the students, clothed in mourning black,
Shall wait upon his heavy funeral.   *Exeunt*

The Tragicall Histoɪ of the Life and Death

of Doctor FAVSTVS.

With new Additions.

Written by *Ch. Mar.*

Printed at London for *Iohn Wright*, and are to be fold at his fhop without Newgate, 1624.